Journey to Freedom

Library of
AFRICAN-AMERICAN HISTORY

Journey to
Freedom

THE AFRICAN-AMERICAN
GREAT MIGRATION

MAURICE ISSERMAN

☑® Facts On File, Inc.

Journey to Freedom: The African-American Great Migration

Copyright © 1997 by Maurice Isserman

Facts On File, Inc.
11 Penn Plaza
New York NY 10001

Poems on p. 38 and p. 75 are from *Collected Poems* by Langston Hughes. Copyright © 1994 by the Estate of Langston Hughes. Reprinted by permission of Alfred A. Knopf Inc.

Lyrics on p. 98 are from "Just a Dream," words and music by Big Bill Broonzy. © Copyright 1939, 1963 by MCA MUSIC PUBLISHING, a Division of UNIVERSAL STUDIOS, INC. Copyright Renewed. International Copyright Secured. All Rights Reserved.

Library of Congress Cataloging-in-Publication Data

Isserman, Maurice.
   Journey to freedom : the African-American great migration /
by Maurice Isserman.
      p.   cm.—(Library of African-American history)
   Includes bibliographical references and index.
   Summary: Discusses the northward journey of Black southerners, the greatest internal mass migration of people in American history.
   ISBN 0-8160-3413-3
   1. Afro-Americans—Migrations—History—20th century—Juvenile literature.
2. Afro-Americans—Southern States—History—20th century—
Juvenile literature. 3. Rural-urban migration—United States—History—
20th century—Juvenile literature. 4. United States—Race relations—Juvenile
literature. [1. Afro-Americans—Southern States. 2. Rural-urban migration.
3. Race relations.]   I. Title.   II. Series.
E185.6.I85   1997
975'.00496073—dc21   96-52160

Text design by Cathy Rincon
Cover design by Nora Wertz
Illustrations on page 57, 68, 81 by Jeremy Eagle/Dale Williams

Printed in the United States of America

MP FOF 10 9 8 7 6 5 4 3 2 1

This book is printed on acid-free paper.

This book is for Mark,

Bobby, Sonia,

Matthew, and Eva

I am grateful to Jamie Warren for having suggested this topic to me, to Nicole Bowen for editorial assistance, and to the reference librarians of Hamilton College for all their diligent efforts in aiding my research.

Contents

Journey to Freedom

1

"Sweet Canaan's Happy Land"

In the midst of the First World War, a group of 147 African-American men, women, and children were traveling together aboard the Illinois Central Railroad, leaving behind their homes in Hattiesburg, Mississippi, for a new life in the North. It was a long day's journey to Chicago. Passengers sat up or tried to sleep on the hard benches of the "Jim Crow"—as segregated black facilities were called—car on the train. Even if they had had the money to purchase better traveling accommodations, there were no sleeping berths in Pullman cars available for blacks on southern trains, nor were they allowed to find seats in the more comfortable and less crowded passenger cars reserved for whites. As the train chugged its way northward from southern Mississippi, through Tennessee and Kentucky, smoke and cinders from the locomotive came through the open windows, for the Jim Crow cars were placed in the least desirable position, at the front of the train just behind the locomotive.

At last they reached the Ohio River and the Illinois state line. Once over the river, they would be leaving the South behind. They had no intention of ever returning. As the train crossed the bridge, the migrants knelt, wept, and prayed. The men took their watches out of their pockets and stopped them to signify the end of their old life and the start of the new. Men, women, and children alike raised their voices in a song of deliverance: "I done come out of the Land of Egypt with the good news. . . ."

The arrival of an African-American family in the "Promised Land" of Chicago during the First World War (Chicago Commission on Race Relations, *The Negro in Chicago*, 1920, p. 92)

The passengers who knelt that day in the Jim Crow train car were a small part of the advance wave of what came to be known as the "Great Migration." From 1916 to 1918 nearly a half million black southerners made the same trek northward; in the decade that followed, three quarters of a million more joined them in the cities of the North. They came by rail, by merchant ship up the east coast—some even came by foot. Like the European immigrants who stepped off the boat at Ellis Island, African-American migrants came as individuals, or in family groups, in quest of a better life in what was for them a new world. The Great Migration is part of the story of the centuries-long struggle of African Americans for freedom, dignity, and equal rights, as well as for basic economic opportunity. The greatest internal mass migration of people in American history, the Great Migration had far-reaching social, economic, and political consequences for the nation as a whole. South and North alike would be transformed in the decades that followed as a result of this vast movement of people seeking "to come out of the Land of Egypt with the good news. . . ."

Like ancient Egypt, the American South had been a land of bondage for people of African descent ever since the first shipment of 20 black captives was unloaded on a dock in Jamestown, in the English colony of Virginia in 1619. By 1808, when by constitutional decree the legal importation of slaves came to an end in the United States, somewhere between 400,000 and 1 million Africans had been forcibly transported to North America. Tens of thousands more were illegally smuggled into the United States in the years leading up to the Civil War.

Slaves were considered to be "chattel," or property, not much different in kind than horses or cows, and could be bought and sold and disposed of at the whim of, and for the profit of, their white masters. Slaves were an expensive commodity, so their owners had an economic incentive to keep them healthy and productive. But otherwise there were few restraints on the absolute power that white masters exercised over black slaves. The southern colonies adopted harsh laws to guarantee the security and profitability of the slave system. Slaves could not leave the plantation without their master's written permission; it was illegal to teach them to read or write; their marriages had no legal standing and could be ended at the discretion of the master; the children of black mothers could be taken from them and sold.

Africans were brought to all the English colonies in North America as slaves; by the time of the American Revolution 50,000 slaves lived in the northern colonies. But slavery was never very important in the northern economy. It was in the South, with its system of plantation agriculture, that the "peculiar institution" set down lasting roots. Slaves tended tobacco in Virginia, rice in South Carolina, and sugarcane in Louisiana. It was with the spread of the cotton crop that their fate was most intimately bound. English and American textile manufacturers were voracious consumers of the staple cotton grown in the South. The slave population of the South was half a million at the time of the American Revolution; by 1860 it had grown to nearly 4 million. Of these, nearly 2 million lived and labored on cotton plantations in a belt stretching from Virginia to Texas.

Thus unlike most Americans of European descent, the ancestors of African Americans did not come to the new world as voluntary immigrants. They had been kidnapped from West African villages, carried by slave ships across the Atlantic, and sold on the docks of West Indian or North American ports. Later generations were traded from master to master, plantation to plantation, with little regard for their personal wishes or family ties. To be "sold down the river" —that is, to be sent farther south—was a dreaded fate, a journey into the unknown undertaken by the unwilling.

What did freedom mean to slaves? The first and most basic definition was control over their own movements. For tens of thousands of slaves in the decades before the Civil War, laying claim to freedom meant becoming a migrant—and a fugitive. The first voluntary African-American migrants were those who escaped from slavery and fled to the northern United States or Canada. Given the penalties that faced failed runaways, including whipping, branding, or worse, it was remarkable that every year thousands ran the risk. Aided by a network of free blacks and sympathetic whites, the "Underground Railroad" delivered perhaps as many as a hundred thousand former slaves to freedom. "Oh, de land I am bound for,/Sweet Canaan's happy land I am bound for," African Americans sang in one of the songs that sustained their spirits under slavery.

"Sweet Canaan's happy land" could be taken as the promise of a better life after death, when all souls were equal before God's eyes in heaven. But it carried another meaning as well, that of deliverance in this world, and through one's own actions. As the African-American sociologist W. E. B. DuBois wrote in *The Souls of Black Folk*, a decade and a half before the start of the Great Migration:

> Through all the sorrow of the Sorrow Songs there breathes a hope—a faith in the ultimate justice of things. The minor cadences of despair change often to triumph and calm confidence. Sometimes it is faith in life, sometimes a faith in death, sometimes assurances of boundless justice in some fair world

Oh, de land I am bound for, Sweet Canaan's happy land I am bound for, Sweet Canaan's happy land I am bound for, Sweet Canaan's happy land, Pray, give me your right hand. Oh, my brother, did you come for to help me, Oh, my sis-ter, did you come for to help me, Oh, my brother, did you come for to help me, Oh, my brother, did you come for to help me Oh, my sis-ter, did you come for to help me, Oh, my sis-ter, did you come for to help me; Pray, give me your right hand, your right hand. Pray, &c.

◆

—Mary F. Armstrong,
Hampton and Its Students (1875)

beyond. But whichever it is, the meaning is always clear: that sometime, somewhere, men will judge men by their souls and not by their skins.

For hundreds of thousands of African Americans during the First World War and the years that followed, that "sometime, somewhere" that DuBois spoke of came to take on the specific and imminently realizable meaning of "as soon as we move to the north."

NOTES

p. 5   "Oh, de land I am bound for . . ." Mary F. Armstrong, *Hampton and Its Students* (New York: Putnam, 1875), p. 62.

p. 5   "Through all the sorrow . . ." W. E. B. DuBois, *The Souls of Black Folk* (New York: New American Library, 1989), p. 274.

2

"Egypt Land": Black Life in the South

At a cost of some 600,000 Union and Confederate dead, the Civil War ended slavery in the United States. The Thirteenth Amendment to the Constitution, adopted in 1865, declared that "neither slavery nor involuntary servitude . . . shall exist within the United States." The Fourteenth and Fifteenth amendments, adopted in 1868 and 1870, extended—at least in theory—the full rights of citizenship, including the right to vote, to all American men, regardless of "race, color, or previous condition of servitude." But after a period of a few years during which the guns of the victorious Union Army reinforced the claim of the newly freed African Americans to their hard-won constitutional rights, the "Reconstruction" of the South

7

came to an abrupt end. With the withdrawal of the remaining occupation forces from South Carolina and Louisiana in 1877, the South's 4 million African Americans were left only a fragile and compromised set of freedoms.

When the guns were stilled in the spring of 1865, the defeated slave owners cherished the dream of reestablishing slavery under another name. Above all, they wanted to prevent the former slaves from moving away from the countryside, where their labor was needed on the plantations, and into the cities, where it was more difficult to maintain control over their activities. In the summer and fall of 1865, southern state legislatures accordingly passed a series of laws known as the "Black Codes." Had these laws been allowed to stand, they would have virtually reinstated slavery as the fate of African Americans. The Black Codes required the freed slaves to sign yearly labor contracts with plantation owners, restricted their movements, and made it illegal for them to rent land. Those who broke their contracts could be punished by whipping or sold for a year's labor. "Vagrancy" statutes were drawn up in ways that would have fastened a new yoke of dependency and forced labor on the necks of blacks.

But the Black Codes proved a failure. The freedmen and -women resisted their reenslavement, and they left the plantations in droves. Although few traveled far from the homes they had known under slavery, they relished the freedom of moving around without anyone's permission, Richard Edwards, a black preacher in northern Florida, urged his followers in 1865 to "shake the dust of the Old Plantation off your feet."

So long as the shadow of the great house falls across you, you ain't going to feel like no free man, and you ain't going to feel like no free woman. You must all move—you must move clear away from the old place what you know, to the new places what you don't know, where you can raise up your head without no fear of

"Marse Dis [This]," or "Marse Tudder [The Other]." Take your freedom, my brothers and sisters. You-all is just as good as anybody, and you-all is just as free! Go where you please—do what you please—forget about the white folks—and now stand up on your feet—lift up your eyes—and shout with me Glory Hallelujah! Amen!

The U.S. Congress in Washington, D.C., under the influence of "Radical Republicans" from the victorious northern states, had no intention of allowing the ex-Confederates to gain back through the Black Codes by stealth what they had lost on the battlefield. During the era of Radical Reconstruction that followed the congressional elections of 1866, Congress enacted a series of constitutional amendments and laws designed to give the vote to and protect the civil rights of southern blacks. The Fourteenth Amendment to the constitution, ratified in 1868, was meant to assure basic rights and equality under the law for all American citizens, regardless of color, and the Fifteenth Amendment, ratified in 1870, declared that no state could discriminate in voting rights based on race. Constitutional amendments, in themselves, guarantee nothing; but for a while the federal government used its powers to ensure that the law of the land was equally respected in all regions. Under the watchful eyes of military occupation forces, and the newly established federal Bureau of Refugees, Freedmen,

Our Government rests upon the broad principle that governments justly exist by the consent of the governed. For that principle the colored men fought with our fathers in the Revolution; and side by side in the fiercest fields of this war they have defended it side by side with our brothers. . . . Do we mean to be just? If we do, we shall give them a vote in the reconstruction of the insurrectionary States.

◆

—from an editorial entitled "The Blacks and the Ballot," in *Harper's Weekly*, May 20, 1865 and Abandoned Lands (better known as the Freedmen's Bureau), African Americans living in the South were able to go to the polls and choose their own representatives. With many whites temporarily disenfranchised because of their support for the Confederacy, blacks formed a majority of the electorate in 1867 in Alabama, Florida, Louisiana, Mississippi, and South Carolina. Sixteen black Republicans were elected to Congress during Reconstruction, and hundreds more won state and local offices.

It was a time of high hopes. Some dreamed that southern blacks, like the white yeoman farmers of New England, New York, Pennsylvania, and the Midwest, would forge new, prosperous, and dignified lives as independent property owners. F. L. Cardozo, a black delegate to the Constitutional Convention of South Carolina in 1868, declared:

> One of the greatest of slavery bulwarks was the infernal plantation system, one man owning his thousand, another his twenty, another fifty thousand acres of land. This is the only way by which we will break up that system, and I maintain that our freedom will be of no effect if we allow it to continue. What is the main cause of the prosperity of the North? It is because every man has his own farm and is free and independent. Let the lands of the South be similarly divided . . .

During the war there had been talk in Washington that the federal government would confiscate the property of slave owners, and that freed slaves would be compensated for their years of servitude with "40 acres and a mule." When the shooting stopped, however, it turned out that most white northern politicians' regard for property rights outweighed their commitment to remaking southern society. By dint of hard work and sacrifice, a minority of freed slaves were able to acquire land of their own. But the great majority remained propertyless. Southern white landowners understood the

A *slave family outside their cabin*   (Special Collections and Archives, W. E. B. DuBois Library, University of Massachusetts, Amherst)

threat that black proprietorship represented to the political and social order, and many refused to sell or rent land to blacks. As F. L. Cardozo had warned, without the economic independence that came with landownership, political rights granted southern blacks proved short-lived.

The economy of the South was indeed remade, but not in the image of the New England countryside. For a while there was a standoff between the desires of the freedmen and those of their former owners. African Americans refused to work as gang laborers on plantations. But the whites still controlled all the land. And so, in the end, a compromise was worked out. White landowners divided their property into smaller parcels, each with its own cabin and fields. Black families moved into the cabins and farmed the land—but did not own it. When the harvest came in, they "shared" the product of their labor with the landowner. Tenant and owner usually each received half the value of the harvest—and thus was born the system that came to be known as "sharecropping."

Sharecropping offered black families some advantages. They were freed from the daily supervision of white overseers. Families could stay together and determine for themselves how to divide up their labor. And, with luck, a good harvest, and a good price for their crops, it was possible to turn a profit at the time of the annual "settle" with the landlord.

But few did make a profit. The price of cotton dropped steadily in the decades after the Civil War, from 30 cents a pound in the 1860s to 6 cents a pound in the 1890s. The sharecroppers, who rarely had any spare cash, paid dearly for credit from white landowners and merchants for the purchase of their seed, fertilizer, food, and clothing, and then were often cheated when it came time for the annual settling.

As if by design—and to an extent it was by design—the sharecroppers often ended up deeper in debt at the end of the year than when they started. Economic intimidation—the threat of being cut off from credit or thrown off the land— proved an effective way for whites to keep blacks from exercising the political rights theoretically guaranteed them by the Thirteenth, Fourteenth, and Fifteenth Amendments to the Constitution.

Where economic pressures were not enough, other kinds of threats reinforced the message. In 1866 a group of ex-Confederate soldiers in Pulaski, Tennessee, founded a secret order known as the Ku Klux Klan (KKK). Within a few years it spread

August 1, 1879

. . . [B]y the help of God we intend to make our start to Kansas land. We had Rather Suffer and be free, than to suffer [the] infamous degrades that are Brought upon us. . . .

Rev. S. Heath
Moses Heath
Lenoir, Co., N.C.

◆

—From a letter to the National Emigrant Aid Society, by a group of prospective "Exodusters" in North Carolina across the South and won a fearsome reputation for violent intimidation. Any time a black man "stepped out of his place"—in a landlord-tenant dispute, or in a political contest—he was at risk of a visit from the Klan or similar groups. Armed Klansmen would ride up to sharecroppers' cabins at night in white, hooded robes and masks. The fortunate ones would get off with a warning: a fiery cross burned outside their cabin. The unlucky would be dragged from their homes, whipped, or in many cases murdered. As a black Republican from Louisiana testified before a congressional committee in 1869:

> There were numerous secret political organizations of the democratic party throughout the parish, known . . . as the "Ku Klux Klans," whose objects were to intimidate the republicans and prevent them from voting at all, unless they would vote the democratic ticket. These organizations were armed with fire-arms and patrolled the parish night and day, committing murders and outrages upon the republicans, and produced such terror and alarm among the freedmen and others belonging to the republican party that it was unsafe for them to hold meetings. . . . Witness knows of a great many freedmen who were republicans, and who desired to vote the republican ticket, who were, by violence, fraud, and intimidation, compelled to vote the democratic ticket. . . . Before and on the day of the election the principal roads in the parish leading to the different places of voting were patrolled by armed men of these Klans for the purpose of intercepting republicans going to vote; and in many instances, plantations where freedmen were employed were guarded by armed men to prevent the freedmen from going to the polls.

The Klan was suppressed by federal troops at the end of the 1860s, temporarily, as it turned out, but the use of terror tactics

Booker T. Washington _____

Born in slavery in western Virginia in 1856, Booker T. Washington rose to a position of great influence as an educator and power broker. With the publication of his widely read autobiography, *Up from Slavery* in 1901, Washington was hailed as a black Benjamin Franklin. Like his 18th-century predecessor, Washington preached a gospel of hard work and self-improvement. In 1881 Washington founded Tuskegee Institute in Alabama, a school devoted to teacher training and industrial education for blacks. With generous support from white northern philanthropists, Tuskegee endowed its students with practical skills and a set of stern moral virtues. Blacks would get nowhere, Washington argued, by directly challenging southern racism. There only hope for advance as individuals and as a race, was to make themselves indispensable to the southern economy. In his famous address delivered at the opening of the Cotton States Exposition in Atlanta, Georgia, on September 18, 1895, Washington promised his white listeners that in the future blacks would refrain from "agitation of questions of social equality." Blacks would remain happily in the South, doing everything they could to win the respect of whites:

> A ship lost at sea for many days suddenly sighted a friendly vessel. From the mast of the unfortunate vessel was seen a signal, "Water,

to regain and enforce white supremacy remained a common practice. Lynch law—unlawful sentences of death, carried out by mobs, to punish the alleged crimes of the victims—ruled in much of the South, particularly in rural areas. Whites as well as blacks were lynched in the United States throughout the 19th century, but increasingly it was a form of punishment reserved for black victims. In 1882, for example, of the 113 people who were lynched that year in the United States, 49 were black and 64 were white. Ten years later, in 1892, of the 230 lynching victims, 161 were black, and 69 were white.

water; we die of thirst!" The answer from the friendly vessel at once came back, "Cast down your bucket where you are." A second time the signal, "Water, water; send us water!" ran up from the distressed vessel, and was answered, "Cast down your bucket where you are." And a third and fourth signal for water was answered, "Cast down your bucket where you are." The captain of the distressed vessel, at last heeding the injunction, cast down his bucket, and it came up full of fresh, sparkling water from the mouth of the Amazon River. To those of my race who depend on bettering their condition in a foreign land or who underestimate the importance of cultivating friendly relations with the Southern white man, who is their next-door neighbor, I would say: "Cast down your bucket where you are"—cast it down in making friends in every manly way of the people of all races by whom we are surrounded.

At the height of his fame in the years after the Cotton States Exposition, Washington enjoyed tremendous political influence. Washington's "Tuskegee Machine" distributed political patronage positions to loyal black supporters on behalf of the Republican party, and was a source of financial subsidy to many black newspapers. Had he lived long enough to witness the Great Migration, it is likely he would have used whatever means were at his disposal to oppose it. Washington had a vested interest in keeping blacks in the South, where his political influence was virtually uncontested. But by the time of his death in 1915, Washington's power had begun to wane. A new generation of black leaders, including such figures as the northern-born and educated W. E. B. DuBois, had come to reject Washington's accomodationist policies. ◆

The lynching of black men was such an accepted practice in the South at the turn of the century that it often turned into a kind of community festival for whites. Large crowds of spectators would turn out to witness the spectacle of a black man being hung or burned at the stake, while white lawmen turned a blind eye when they did not actually participate.

Through such methods, and with the waning of northern interest in the fate of the freedmen, white "redeemers" soon overturned most of the Reconstruction state governments in the South. By 1877 the region's experiment with interracial democracy was over. In the decades that followed, white supremacy was enshrined in southern state law. Poll taxes and restrictive voter registration practices were used to selectively disenfranchise southern black voters. The Louisiana constitution of 1897 was typical, with stringent literacy requirements for voting, which could be waived if a voter's grandfather had been eligible to vote on January 1, 1867 or had served in the Confederate or United States Army, known as the "grandfather clause." The measure, as intended, effectively excluded blacks from the polls—the number of registered black voters in the state dropped from over 130,000 in 1896 to just over 5,000 in 1900.

At the same time, southern state legislatures passed laws enforcing racial segregation in public accommodations and public conveyances. "For whites only" and "for colored only" signs went up all over the South. Blacks and whites were required by law to ride in separate cars on trains and in separate seating sections on streetcars. Waiting rooms, restaurants, hotels, public toilets, elevators, public tele-

Black school in the rural South   (Special Collections and Archives, W. E. B. DuBois Library, University of Massachusetts, Amherst)

phones, and water fountains all fell under the new, strict system of Jim Crow segregation. In 1896, Jim Crow received the blessing of the U.S. Supreme Court. In a case growing out of a Louisiana law requiring segregated seating on railroads, *Plessy* v. *Ferguson*, the Court held that segregation was lawful so long as the facilities provided both races were "separate but equal." It did not trouble the Court that in reality the resources provided blacks were inevitably inferior. In South Carolina's system of public education, for example, the expenditure for each white pupil at the turn of the century was six times that offered the equivalent black pupil.

Thus in the last decades of the 19th century, southern blacks found themselves treated as a despised social caste, denied the most basic rights of citizens, and locked into a condition of seemingly perpetual debt, poverty, malnutrition, ill health, and ignorance. Racism was enshrined, not only in custom and law, but in respectable opinion—both in the South and the North. A "scientific racism," based on pseudo-Darwinist notions of the "survival of the fittest" and promoted by prominent historians, sociologists, and anthropologists, was used to justify racial inequality. And the most prominent black spokesman of the era, educator Booker T. Washington, urged a policy of accommodation to racial inequality.

A small but steady stream of African Americans left the South in the first decades after the Civil War in hopes of finding a better life in the North or the West. Between 1870 and 1910, roughly 7,000 blacks migrated every year. Most left as individuals, or families, or in small groups. But in the spring of 1879, a mass migration movement with a common destination—Kansas—sprang up in black communities in Louisiana and Mississippi. Amid great excitement, perhaps 10,000 or more blacks set out for what they believed was the promised land, with freedom and abundant opportunity. Comparing themselves to the Jews escaping Pharaoh in biblical times, they called themselves the "Exodusters."

Kansas did not turn out to be a land of milk and honey for the Exodusters. Many arrived with no more than the clothes on their backs, and most remained as impoverished as they had been in the South. White southern landowners, alarmed at the prospect of losing their labor force, did what they could to discourage would-be migrants. The movement soon died out. But it proved a harbinger of things to come.

NOTES

p. 8 "So long as the shadow . . ." Richard Edwards, quoted in Leon F. Litwack, *Been in the Storm So Long: The Aftermath of Slavery* (New York: Vintage, 1980), p. 296.

p. 10 "One of the greatest . . ." F. L. Cardozo, quoted in Walter L. Fleming, ed., *Documentary History of Reconstruction*, Vol. I (New York: McGraw-Hill, 1966), p. 450.

p. 13 "There were numerous secret . . ." Quoted in Walter L. Fleming, ed., *Documentary History of Reconstruction*, Vol. II (New York: McGraw-Hill, 1966), p. 370.

p. 14 "A ship lost at sea . . ." Booker T. Washington, *Up from Slavery* (New York: Airmont Books, 1967), p. 134.

3

"Unreconciled Strivings": Black Life in the North

"How does it feel to be a problem?" the African-American scholar W. E. B. DuBois asked in the introduction to his 1903 collection of essays, *The Souls of Black Folk*. For black Americans, he argued, it created a sense of "double-consciousness":

> One ever feels his two-ness,—an American, a Negro; two souls, two thoughts, two unreconciled strivings; two warring ideals in one dark body. . . .

DuBois, born in Great Barrington, Massachusetts, in 1868, had never known slavery and did not experience the full brunt of racial prejudice until he enrolled as a student at

W. E. B. DuBois, 1915   (Special Collections and Archives, W. E. B. DuBois Library, University of Massachusetts, Amherst)

Fisk University in Nashville, Tennessee in 1885. His sense of "being a problem" thus came to him gradually. But it would guide his scholarship and his political activism over the course of an enormously productive 70-year career. His achievements included the first scientific study of a northern urban black community, *The Philadelphia Negro*, published in 1899.

African-American life in the urban North as in the rural South was, in DuBois' term, a source of "unreconciled strivings." For slaves in the prewar South, the North had been the promised land of freedom. But the nearly quarter million African Americans living in the North at the time of the Civil War, though free of slavery's chains, knew that their acceptance as free and equal citizens of the republic was by no means assured. Northern whites may have opposed slavery, or at least its further territorial expansion, but not primarily out of sympathy or fellowship for blacks. White workingmen, including many immigrants who were themselves the target of prejudice and discrimination, feared the economic competition of black laborers. In the 1830s and 1840s race riots broke out in Boston, New York, Philadelphia, Cleveland, and Cincinnati. As a result of discrimination and poverty, what would later be called "ghettos" were already emerging in northern cities in the prewar era, and were notorious for overcrowding, disease, and crime.

Although slavery was abolished in the North in the early 19th century, most northern states maintained discriminatory "black laws" on their books, restricting the rights of blacks to vote, to serve on juries, to attend public schools, or even to settle. Some northern states erected legal barriers to black immigration. White northerners feared the possibility that black equality would lead to social mixing and interracial marriages.

In many ways, ironically, the free states of the prewar North offered a preview of what life would be like for the freed slaves in the post-Reconstruction South. Black abolitionist leader Frederick Douglass lived in Lynn, Massachusetts, in the 1840s, and later wrote of this period:

> My treatment in the use of public conveyances about these times was extremely rough, especially on the Eastern Railroad, from Boston to Portland [Maine]. On that road, as on many others, there was a mean, dirty, and uncomfortable car set apart for colored travellers called the Jim Crow car. Regarding this as the fruit of slaveholding prejudice and being determined to fight the spirit of slavery wherever I might find it, I resolved to avoid this car, though it sometimes required some courage to do so. . . . I . . . sometimes was soundly beaten by the conductor and brakeman. On one occasion six of these "fellows of the baser sort," under the direction of the conductor, set out to eject me from my seat. As usual, I had purchased a first-class ticket and paid the required sum for it, and on the requirement of the

—VOL. I. NO. 5.—

THE
AMERICAN
ANTI-SLAVERY
ALMANAC,

FOR

1840,

BEING BISSEXTILE OR LEAP-YEAR, AND THE 64TH OF AMERICAN
INDEPENDENCE.   CALCULATED FOR NEW YORK; ADAPTED
TO THE NORTHERN AND MIDDLE STATES.

Slave State   *Free State*

NORTHERN HOSPITALITY—NEW YORK NINE MONTHS' LAW.
The slave steps out of the slave-state, and his chains fall.   A free state, with another
chain, stands ready to re-enslave him.

Thus saith the Lord, Deliver him that is spoiled out of the hands of the oppressor.

NEW YORK:
PUBLISHED BY THE AMERICAN ANTI-SLAVERY SOCIETY,
NO. 143 NASSAU STREET.

Front page of The American Anti-Slavery Almanac, 1840   (New-York
Historical Society)

conductor to leave, refused to do so. . . . They . . . found me much attached to my seat, and in removing me I tore away two or three of the surrounding ones, on which I held with a firm grasp, and did the car no service in some other respects. . . . The result was that Stephen A. Chase, superintendent of the road, ordered all passenger trains to pass through Lynn, where I then lived, without stopping.

Blacks were not the only group to experience hard times in American cities in the 19th century. In the early and mid-19th century, successive waves of European immigrants arrived on American shores, many of them from Ireland and Germany. They did not find the streets paved with gold. Hard physical labor, low wages, and recurrent unemployment were the fate of millions of newly arrived immigrants. Still, as newer groups of immigrants arrived, longer-established ethnic communities found it possible to rise up the scale of income and social acceptance. Starting at the end of the 19th century, the main source of new immigrants shifted to southern and eastern Europe, including Italy, Poland, Hungary, Russia, and Greece. At the height of the "new immigration," between 1901 and 1910, about a million immigrants entered the United States each year. By 1910, one third of the nation's population were either immigrants or had one or more immigrant parents.

Some optimistic well-wishers argued that black migrants to northern cities would benefit from the same process of gradual ethnic assimilation experienced by European immigrants. That argument overlooked the fact that blacks were hardly newcomers. Long before the arrival of the Irish and the Germans and the Italians and the Jews, Africans and their descendants were living in the cities of the Northeast and Midwest. In 1623, the first black slaves were brought by the Dutch settlers to New Amsterdam—the city that after its capture by the English in 1664 was renamed New York. By

1746 more than a fifth of New York City's population was black. The first non–Native American settler in the region that the Potawatomi Indians of Illinois referred to as "Chickagou"—which later became the city of Chicago—was a French-speaking trader of black ancestry named Jean-Baptiste Pointe du Sable. Property records show that blacks already owned houses in Chicago when the city was officially incorporated in 1837.

The black population of both cities continued to grow in succeeding years. In 1860 there were over 12,000 black residents of New York City, and about 1,000 in Chicago. Fifty years later, on the eve of the Great Migration, those numbers had increased to over 90,000 in New York City, and over 40,000 in Chicago. By then three northern cities —New York, Philadelphia, and Chicago—were counted among the top ten largest black communities in the nation.

Given the conditions prevailing in the South in the late 19th century, it may seem surprising that black migrants relocating in the North could be counted in tens rather than hundreds of thousands. But with a steady influx of European immigrants willing to work long hours for low pay in unskilled factory jobs, there was little incentive for northern industrial employers to encourage black migration. At the

Centers of African-American Urban Population, 1910	
Washington, D.C.	94,446
New York City	91,709
New Orleans	89,262
Baltimore	84,749
Philadelphia	84,459
Memphis	52,441
Birmingham	52,305
Atlanta	51,902
Richmond	46,733
Chicago	44,103
	Source: U.S. Census data, 1910

same time, skilled white craftsmen in the North did their best to make sure that blacks could not find work in the better-paying trades. It was easier for a black man to work as a carpenter in New Orleans than in New York.

Although northern cities were home to a small black middle class of doctors, lawyers, druggists, ministers, and small businessmen at the turn of the century, most blacks were kept at the margins of the urban economy. Black men could find jobs as waiters, porters, janitors, or barbers; black women as laundresses and domestic servants. If anything, black women had a much easier time earning a living than did black men, and this in an era when very few white women worked outside the home. A survey taken in 1910 showed that over 30 percent of married black women in New York City worked, compared to little over 4 percent of white women. Mary White Ovington, a white reformer, was among the first to describe this phenomenon. Ovington's parents had been abolitionists, and she grew up hearing stories of the heroism of those northerners who helped slaves escape along the Underground Railroad in the years before the Civil War. Decades later, she decided to see what she could do on behalf of the children and grandchildren of the slave generation. She undertook an investigation of "The Negro Home in New York" on behalf of the Greenwich House settlement house, and her findings were published in the journal *Charities* in 1905:

> [A]nother aspect of the Negro home that is of great importance [is] the presence of the mother as a wage-earner. Some-

> *Beneficial societies in endless number are formed here; secret societies keep in touch; co-operative and building associations have lately sprung up; the minister often acts as an employment agent; considerable charitable and relief work is done and special meetings held to aid special projects.*
>
> ◆
>
> —W. E. B. DuBois, 1899

Mary White Ovington (Special Collections and Archives, W. E. B. DuBois Library, University of Massachusetts, Amherst)

times the woman of the household earns more money than the man; often she earns as much. Her most profitable employment is domestic service, but this takes her away from her home for eight or ten, even for fourteen hours of the day. Many a mother, feeling that she cannot leave her children for the most of their waking hours, engages in the chief home industry of the colored woman, washing. In this she is an expert and her laundry commands good prices; but it turns her home into a workshop and makes her few rooms hotter, more cluttered, more unhealthful. . . . The work is unendingly wearying, lasting often into the night, and it results in a smaller wage than can be obtained with less expenditure of time in a workshop.

The colored men who work on the railroads and on the boats, or who go as waiters to the large hotels, are absent from their families for much of the year. They have little part in the care and rearing of their children. Others, such as the night watchmen and the hotel men, have some of their leisure in the daytime and can give more attention to the children than is possible with many fathers. Parental feeling is often strong among the Negro men. . . .

It may be said, however, with some certainty, that the economic situation of the New York Negro does not lead to a strengthening of the home life and of the marriage tie. The economic independence of the woman and the frequent absence from home of the man lead to desertions and separations. The attractive woman who is able to care for herself may grow to resent the presence of a husband whose support she does not need, and the lazy man may find another woman than his wife to support him. The presence of lodgers, necessitated by a high rent, is also a cause of loose family life. That there are many separated families among the poorer class of colored people all charitable workers know, and the woman's economic independence coupled with the man's inability to earn a good wage does something to promote such a condition.

Not content to be an outside observer, Ovington would move into a block of model tenements constructed in the black neighborhood of New York City known as San Juan Hill. She was the only white resident on the entire block. Her sympathies would in time lead her to become one of the founding members of the National Association for the Advancement of Colored People (NAACP).

As Ovington and other reformers recognized, economic competition between the races was among the chief sources of racial animosity. New York City's history provided bloody proof of that proposition. In July 1863, white workingmen in New York, many of them Irish-Americans, rioted in protest of draft laws that allowed the rich to escape military service in the Civil War. The riots quickly took on a racist character, because the workers feared that once the war was over, hordes of freed blacks would move North and take their jobs. The rioters murdered dozens of New York City's black residents and burned down the Colored Orphan Asylum before battle-hardened federal troops were sent into the city to put down the uprising.

With the growth of manufacturing, new technologies displaced skilled craftsmen with unskilled workers, and small workshops with great factories. Workers felt they were increasingly at a disadvantage in dealing with their employers. In 1869 the *New York Times* ran a series of articles exploring the conditions of "our working classes." While deploring the spread of strikes and trade unions, the *Times* described the plight of the average worker in a large industrial establishment as being

> a system of slavery as absolute if not as degrading as that which lately prevailed at the South. The only difference is that there agriculture was the field, landed proprietors were the masters and negroes were the slaves; while in the North manufacturers is the field, manufacturing capitalists threaten to become the masters, and it is the white laborers who are to be slaves.

Notwithstanding the obvious exaggerations of this comparison, northern white workers anxiously faced economic hardship and an uncertain future in the new industrial system. There were some who urged the labor movement to recognize that the former chattel slaves of the South, and the "wage slaves" of the North, should make common cause. Isaac Myers, a skilled black worker from Baltimore, spoke before the convention of the National Labor Union (NLU) in Philadelphia in 1869. (The NLU was the first of several attempts in the post–Civil War era to unite all labor unions in the United States in a common federation.) Myers urged the mostly white audience in attendance to accept black workers into their unions on an equal basis:

> I speak today for the colored men of the whole country . . . when I tell you that all they ask for themselves is a fair chance; that you shall be no worse off by giving them that chance; that you and they will dwell in peace and harmony together. . . . The white men of the country have nothing to fear from the colored laboring man. We desire to see labor elevated and made respectable; we desire to have the highest rate of wages that our labor is worth. . . . And you, gentlemen, may rely on the support of the colored laborer of this country in bringing about this result. . . . American citizenship with the black man is a complete failure, if he is proscribed from the workshops of this country.

But Myers' plea fell on deaf ears. The NLU convention instead limited black workers to separate organizations, which could then, if they chose to, affiliate with the NLU. This was Jim Crow in the guise of working-class solidarity. At the turn of the century, the NLU's successor, the American Federation of Labor (AFL), adopted a similar policy of creating separate "federal" union locals for black workers.

Thus it was a matter of no small consequence for the future of American race relations that when black males did find relatively well-paying employment in the North in the years after the war, it was often by necessity in the role of strikebreakers in industrial conflicts. In the 1870s, mine owners in Ohio, Illinois, and Indiana began importing blacks from the border states to take the place of striking white coal miners. In the 1880s and 1890s southern blacks were recruited by Pennsylvania steel mills for the same purpose. In two of the most notorious episodes, thousands of black workers were imported by rail to Chicago to break a strike in the city's stockyards in 1904, and then again the following year to break a teamsters' strike. In many of these instances, blacks weren't told beforehand that they were coming in to take the jobs of other workers. Some, on learning the truth, refused to cross the strike lines. But since unions of the era by and large excluded blacks from membership, calls for labor solidarity did not always inspire the same sympathetic response. Black strikebreaking, of course, only added to the hostility that already divided white and black workers—a factor that worked much to the advantage of employers

Gainfully Occupied African-American Population in the United States in 1910*		
Industry	Number	Percentage
Agriculture, forestry, etc.	2,893,674	55.7
Domestic and personal service	1,074,543	20.7
Manufacturing and mechanical trades	657,130	12.6
Transportation	276,648	5.3
Trade	132,019	2.5
Professional service	69,471	1.3
Public service	26,295	0.5
Others	62,755	1.4
Total United States	5,192,535	
* Ten years of age and older	*Source*: U.S. Census data, 1910	

while sowing the seeds for dramatic outbreaks of racial violence in the future.

At the start of the 20th century, after a century of rapid and often chaotic economic growth, Americans began to take a closer and concerned look at some of the social consequences of industrial and urban development. Historians use the term *progressivism* to describe a variety of movements that after 1900 devoted themselves to improving social conditions. Progressives believed that the scientific investigation of social problems, the arousal of the conscience of the middle class, and enlightened government reform and regulation could do away with such evils as child labor, unsanitary housing, and political corruption.

Progressives were not, however, all of one mind on every issue, including the question of race relations. Southern white Progressives, with few exceptions, were staunch supporters of white supremacy. Northern white Progressives, although deeply interested in the plight of European immigrants in New York, Chicago, and other metropolitan centers, often ignored the plight of the immigrants' black neighbors.

But some Progressives were determined to bring to the urban black community the same kind of scientific study, sympathy, and reform that others devoted to immigrant neighborhoods. Much of what we know today about black urban life on the eve of the Great Migration comes from the writings of white Progressives: Ray Stannard Baker's *Following the Color Line* (1908), Mary White Ovington's *Half a Man: The Status of the Negro in New York* (1911), Louise de Koven Bowen's *Colored People of Chicago* (1913), and John Daniel's *In Freedom's Birthplace: a History of the Boston Negro* (1914). The model and pioneer in this field of research, however, was the black sociologist W. E. B. DuBois.

Urban black communities on the eve of the Great Migration were plagued by problems of unemployment and poverty, disease, and crime. But within these communities there

W. E. B. DuBois _____

W. E. B. DuBois was born in Great Barrington, Massachusetts, in 1868, and educated at Fisk University (1885–88), Harvard University (1888–96), and the University of Berlin (1892–94). He went on to a 70-year career in which he distinguished himself as a historian, sociologist, editor, and political activist.

In 1896 DuBois, then teaching at Ohio's Wilberforce University in Ohio, was invited by the University of Pennsylvania to undertake a study of the black community in Philadelphia. Philadelphia had the North's largest black community in the 1890s, some 40,000 strong. It was a city with a long tradition of abolitionist sentiment due to its Quaker heritage, but also a history of racial hostility and riots.

DuBois agreed to move to the city, and the book he produced, The Philadelphia Negro (1899), is a path-breaking sociological study of African-American urban life that still bears reading a century later. DuBois personally conducted interviews with the members of approximately 2,500 households in the city's Seventh Ward, home to a quarter of Philadelphia's African Americans. DuBois wrote candidly, and sometimes paternalistically, of the crime, vice, and social dislocation that was part of daily life in the Seventh Ward. He urged blacks to reform their own behavior when it reflected a "careless moral training." But he also added a stern admonition to whites inclined to hold blacks solely responsible for their own poverty: "How long can a city teach its black children that the road to success is to have a white face?" he asked.

> There is no doubt that in Philadelphia the center and kernel of the Negro problem so far as the white people are concerned is the narrow opportunities afforded Negroes for earning a decent living. Such

were also dedicated groups and agencies working to bring social change and self-improvement.

One of the most significant institutions created by Progressive reformers at the end of the 19th and the beginning of the 20th century was the settlement house. These were community centers created under private auspices in poor discrimination is morally wrong, politically dangerous, industrially wasteful, and socially silly. It is the duty of the whites to stop it, and to do so primarily for their own sakes. Industrial freedom of opportunity has by long experience been proven to be generally best for all. Moreover the cost of crime and pauperism, the growth of slums, and the pernicious influences of idleness and lewdness, cost the public far more than would the hurt to the feelings of a carpenter to work beside a black man, or a shop-girl to stand beside a darker mate. This does not contemplate the wholesale replacing of white workmen for Negroes out of sympathy or philanthropy; it does mean that talent should be rewarded, and aptness used in commerce and industry whether its owner be black or white; that the same incentive to good, honest, effective work be placed before a black office boy as before a white one—before a black porter as before a white one; and that unless this is done the city has no right to complain that black boys lose interest in work and drift into idleness and crime. . . .

DuBois also offered some pioneering insights in the study of black migration. He noted that most of the southern migrants who came to Philadelphia had made intermediate stops. Rarely did they move directly from the countryside to the big city. A far more typical pattern was to first move to a small southern town or city, and then to move on to the North.

The publication of *The Philadelphia Negro* helped secure DuBois' reputation as the foremost black intellectual of his generation. By the time the book appeared in 1899, DuBois had already moved on to the University of Atlanta, where he would remain for 12 productive years. It was during this period that his most famous work, *The Souls of Black Folk* (1903), appeared with its challenge to Booker T. Washington's racial accommodationism and its famous prediction that "the problem of the 20th century is the problem of the color line." ◆

neighborhoods. Settlement workers, who lived as residents in the houses, offered their neighbors such services as nurseries and kindergartens, cultural programs, coffee houses, vocational training, and much more. Trade unions, debating societies, and boys' and girls' clubs used the settlement houses as meeting places. Well-known settlement houses serving black urban communities at the turn of the century included the Wendell Phillips settlement, the Frederick Douglass Center, and the Abraham Lincoln Centre in Chicago; Stillman House and Green House in New York City; Robert Gould Shaw House in Boston; and Karamu House in Cleveland.

The National Association of Colored Women (NACW), founded in 1896, was a network of black women's clubs and was led for many years by Mary Church Terrell, a prominent Washington, D.C. educator. The clubwomen, drawn largely from the black urban middle class, set up kindergartens, orphanages, homes for the elderly, and for young working women. Another important organization in the black community, the National League on Urban Conditions among Negroes (later and better known as the Urban League), was established in 1910. Headquartered in New York, by 1920 it had 32 branches nationwide. The Urban League provided industrial training for black migrants and aided them in finding jobs and housing. The Young Men's Christian Association (YMCA) and Young Women's Christian Association (YWCA) had been founded in the 19th century to look after the spiritual and physical well-being of young people, particularly those moving to and facing the dangers and temptation of the cities. Although largely a white organization on the national level, it maintained affiliates in black urban communities as well as white, staffed and often directed by African Americans. On Chicago's South Side, both the YMCA and YWCA had active programs, providing housing, meals, industrial training, and recreational opportunities for thousands of black men and women.

Without question, the most long-standing and powerful force holding together the urban black community in the face of adversity were the churches. The creation of the independent black church was one of the most significant achievements of the northern black community in the 19th century. In the prewar South, masters taught slaves a highly selective version of Christianity, emphasizing meekness and submission to authority as the chief lessons to be learned from Scripture. Masters feared and attempted to suppress any attempts at independent black worship, although slaves often drew their own independent conclusions about the true meaning of the biblical stories they were told. In the North, blacks were free to learn to read and write and interpret the Bible for themselves. They were quick to note that the Old Testament was filled with stories of the trials and persecution of the Hebrews, and also of their final triumph over Pharaoh and other oppressors.

If, as both the Old and New Testaments suggested, all believers in biblical times were equal in the eyes of God, then it was easy to draw the further conclusion that all peoples in present times were equally deserving of respectful and equal treatment by secular authorities. But to realize that goal of equality, blacks were first going to have to create their own institutions. In the North many of the established churches discouraged black attendance or maintained separate "Negro pews." In November 1787 the previously integrated St. George Methodist Church in Philadelphia began a policy of segregating its black and white parishioners. Outraged, the blacks withdrew and formed the Free African Society. In 1793 one of their leaders, Richard Allen, organized the Bethel African Methodist Episcopal Church. In 1816, at a gathering of delegates in Philadelphia, a national African Methodist Episcopal (AME) denomination was founded. African-American Baptists founded their own national association of churches around the same time. Within a few decades over 300 independent black congregations were founded in the North. In the prewar era the black churches played an important role in the abolitionist movement. And after emancipation the churches continued the tradition of social activism and practical philanthropy.

At the start of the 20th century, Americans were optimistic that they could solve the social problems that they had

Cover of the June 1918 issue of the NAACP journal The Crisis, *edited by* W. E. B. DuBois   (Special Collections and Archives, W. E. B. DuBois Library, University of Massachusetts, Amherst)

inherited from the 19th century. Acting on that belief, in 1909 a group of prominent Progressive reformers founded the National Association for the Advancement of Colored

People. Mary White Ovington was one of the organizers, and W. E. B. DuBois moved to New York to edit the new association's newletter, *The Crisis*. These progressive reformers were convinced that through a combination of scientific study, journalistic "muckraking," and legal challenges to segregationist statutes, they would reveal to Americans the fundamental irrationality of racist beliefs, and thus diminish and in time eliminate the racial divide in American society.

African Americans were coming to northern cities at a time of great change. Throughout the 19th century, American cities had grown enormously, and without much thought about how to make them livable communities. The Progressives proposed to address those shortcomings, and they were remarkably successful in developing new laws and legislation that made life better for many urban residents, particularly those who lived in the less affluent quarters. Of course, many people still lived in substandard housing, the sanitation in many neighborhoods was unhealthful, and many children lacked decent educational and recreational facilities. The list of the shortcomings of American cities could go on and on. But the important point is that Americans generally felt positive about the future of their cities during the Progressive era. Many still paid homage to the founding myth of the frontier as the source of American progress and democracy. But at the turn of the century, some of the glamor of the frontier had attached itself to America's urban centers. Cities were now seen as dynamic, exciting places to live, full of enterprise,

E*ver since the war, New York has been receiving the overflow of colored population from the Southern cities. In the last decade this migration has grown to such proportions that it is estimated that our Blacks have quite doubled in number. . . . There is no more clean and orderly community in New York than the new settlement of colored people that is growing up on the East Side from Yorkville to Harlem.*

◆

—Jacob Riis, 1890

creativity, and opportunity. The poet Carl Sandburg was one of those who sympathized with the goals of the Progressive reformers, and his famous 1914 tribute to Chicago captured the mood of optimism that defined the American attitude to the city on the eve of the African-American Great Migration:

> Laughing the stormy, husky, brawling laughter of Youth, half-naked, sweating, proud to be Hog Butcher, Tool Maker, Stacker of Wheat, Player with Railroads and Freight Handler to the Nation.

A young black man and aspiring poet named Langston Hughes was among those who admired Sandburg's poem ("I know a lover of life sings," Hughes would write, "When Carl Sandburg sings.") Born in Missouri, raised in Kansas, Hughes would be among the millions who would make a new life for himself in the cities of the North after the Great Migration. "So now I seek the North," he would write in his famous poem "The South," published in DuBois' journal *The Crisis* in 1922:

> The cold-faced North,
> For she, they say,
> Is a kinder mistress,
> And in her house my children
> May escape the spell of the South.

NOTES

p. 19 "One ever feels his two-ness . . ." W. E. B. DuBois, *The Souls of Black Folk* (New York: New American Library, 1982), p. 45.

p. 21 "My treatment in the use of . . ." Frederick Douglass, quoted in Mary Frances Berry and John W. Blassingame, *Long Memory: The Black Experience in America* (New York: Oxford University Press, 1982), p. 59.

p. 25 "[A]nother aspect of the Negro home . . ." Mary White Ovington, "The Negro Home in New York," *Charities*, 15 (October 7, 1905), p. 27.

p. 28 "a system of slavery as absolute . . ." *New York Times*, February 22, 1869.

p. 29 "I speak today for the colored men . . ." *New York Times*, August 19, 1869.

p. 32 "There is no doubt that in Philadelphia . . ." W. E. B. DuBois, *The Philadelphia Negro; a social study* (New York: Schocken Books, 1967), pp. 394–95.

p. 38 "Laughing the stormy, husky, brawling laughter . . ." Carl Sandburg, "Chicago," in Rebecca West, ed., *Selected Poems of Carl Sandburg* (New York: Harcourt, Brace and Co., 1926), p. 29.

p. 38 "The cold-faced North . . ." Arnold Rampersad and David Roessel, *The Collected Poems of Langston Hughes* (New York: Alfred A. Knopf, 1995), p. 27.

4

"The Great Northern Drive": Leaving the South

In August 1914, Britain, France, and Russia went to war with Germany and the Austro-Hungarian Empire in a conflict that became known in time as the First World War. The United States, for the moment, remained neutral. In accord with the long tradition of American isolation from Europe's wars, President Woodrow Wilson pledged that Americans would strive to be "impartial in thought as well as in action." The war soon settled down into a bloody stalemate in the trenches of the western front in France and Belgium, as soldiers on both sides suffered heavy casualties from such deadly innovations of mass destruction as machine guns and poison gas. In 1916,

Wilson won reelection to the White House on the slogan "He kept us out of war."

W. E. B. DuBois, who by this time was widely regarded as the leading African-American spokesperson for the cause of equal rights, was among those appalled by the spectacle of the European slaughter. As a young scholar, he had studied in Germany and retained fond memories of his stay in that country. But he knew that Americans would not remain impartial in the war. Inevitably, the United States was going to be drawn into the conflict. The only question was what, if any, good could come out of all the bloodshed.

DuBois interpreted the war as yet another tragedy produced by "the color line." In an essay published in the spring of 1915, DuBois argued that the conflict in Europe was, basically, a product of the competition for colonial possessions in Africa, Asia, and elsewhere. Europe's profits from colonial exploitation in the 19th and early 20th century had been great, but now the bill was coming due. Future global conflicts could be avoided, DuBois argued, only if "European civilization" extended the "democratic ideal to the yellow, brown, and black peoples" of the world.

Starting with the Spanish-American War in 1898, the United States had also taken part in that scramble for overseas outposts. Notwithstanding President Wilson's proclamation of neutrality, global strategic and economic interests steadily pushed the United States toward involvement in the conflict raging in Europe. Although the war at first disrupted international trade, currency exchange, and credits, it soon proved a boon to the American economy. In 1913–1914 the United States had been suffering from a severe economic downturn, but prosperity returned in matter of months as the country became the granary and arsenal for the Allies. American trade with Britain and France quadrupled between 1914 and 1916. The demand for cotton and wheat spelled good times for American farmers, while in the industrial cities American workers enjoyed full employment and rising wages.

But new opportunities also brought new risks. The Germans hoped to starve Britain into submission by sealing off imports of food and other materials to that island nation. In 1915 they began a campaign of submarine warfare against Allied merchant ships in the Atlantic. Among the casualties of the German "U-boats" were 124 American civilians traveling on a British passenger ship, the *Lusitania*, sunk in May 1915. Outraged protests from the U.S. government led to Germany's temporary suspension of the attacks. But when the German high command decided to resume unrestricted submarine warfare early in 1917, it became only a matter of time before the United States entered the war—particularly since the U-boats were now targeting American as well as British merchant vessels. On April 2, President Wilson asked Congress for a declaration of war; four days later, despite the opposition of some antiwar congressional representatives, he got it.

African-American leaders were divided in their response. Some saw no point in supporting a war for "self-determination" abroad, while blacks were denied the most elementary rights of American citizenship at home. Others like DuBois welcomed American entry into the war. Whatever the intentions of the southern-born President Wilson, who was ordinarily no friend of the cause of civil rights, DuBois believed that the war would bring in its wake new opportunities for African Americans. After all, he reasoned, the enlistment of black soldiers in the Union cause during the Civil War had been one of the factors leading to Lincoln's decision to issue the Emancipation Proclamation. DuBois hoped that black participation in the American war effort in Europe would lead to similar political and legal advances. All told, over 350,000 African Americans wound up serving in the U.S. military during the First World War. DuBois personally, although unsuccessfully, sought a commission as an army

A *meeting of African-American leaders to support the war effort, Washington,* D.C., 1918. (W. E. B. *DuBois is the fourth figure from the left in the first row.*) (Special Collections and Archives, W. E. B. DuBois Library, University of Massachusetts, Amherst)

officer. And in a controversial editorial published in *The Crisis*, the newsletter of the NAACP, DuBois declared:

> Let us, while this war lasts, forget our special grievances and close our ranks shoulder to shoulder with our white fellow citizens and the allied nations that are fighting for democracy.

In later years, bitterly disappointed at the ill treatment of black American soldiers during the war (most of whom were put to hard labor in segregated units under white command), DuBois would come to regret his advice to "close ranks." The war did not result in interracial democracy at home or abroad. But there is no question that the First World War had an enormous impact on black America. The war ushered in an era of change more dramatic than anything that had happened to black Americans since emancipation and Reconstruction. The effects of the war began to be felt long before the first American soldiers embarked for the western front.

The First World War was a time of beginnings and endings. Among the things that came to an end in 1914–1918 was the era of mass European immigration to the United States. From 1900 through 1914, an average of more than a million immigrants a year arrived on American shores. In 1913–1914, with war clouds gathering over the continent, nearly two and a half million Europeans crossed the Atlantic. Then suddenly, with the outbreak of the war and the closing of European borders, the flood was reduced to a trickle. By 1918, a mere hundred thousand immigrants made the journey across the U-boat-infested Atlantic. The young men who would have left Russia, Poland, Hungary, and Italy for jobs in New York, Pittsburgh, and Chicago, were being drafted by their homeland's armies and sent off to the trenches, while their families endured the privations of the home front.

This abrupt end of European immigration had ominous implications for American industry. In 1914, a quarter of the total American work force, and a majority of the work force in heavy industry, was foreign born. Many immigrant workers already in the United States returned to their homelands after 1914 out of a sense of patriotic obligation to take part in the fighting. So at the very moment when the demand for American manufactured goods was skyrocketing, the supply of new recruits to American mines, mills, and factories was drastically reduced. When the United States introduced military conscription in the spring of 1917, and the first of 4 million men left civilian life for wartime military service, the shortage in the workforce grew even more threatening.

Someone, somewhere, was going to have to be found to take up the slack.

And someone was available for the task, not far away and eager to be found. "Dear sir," a black resident of New Orleans wrote to the editor of the *Chicago Defender* in the spring of 1917, with uncertain spelling but obvious sincerity:

> Reading a article in the . . . *Chicago Defender* about the trouble you had to obtain men for work out of Chicago and also seeing a advertisement for men in Detroit saying to apply to you I beg to state to you that if your could secure me a position in or around Chicago or any northern section with fairly good wages & good living conditions for myself and family I will gladly take same. . . . as I said before I will gladly take position in northern city or county where a mans a man. . . . [H]ere are a few position which I am capable of holding down. Laborer, [experienced] porter, butler or driver of Ford car. Tha[n]king you in advance for your kindness. . . .

The "pull" that set the Great Migration in motion was the wartime scarcity of labor for northern industry, plus the enormous disparity in wages offered in the two regions. In the South, the wages that a black worker could earn varied from 40 to 75 cents a day on a farm to perhaps as high as $1.75 in the city. At the same time, wages for unskilled labor in the North paid from $3.00 to $8.00 a day. Living costs were also higher, to be sure, but the prospect of earning in a day in the North what would take a week to earn in the South was hard to resist. And not only were wages significantly higher, but they were also paid on a regular, usually weekly basis, and in cash. For a people used to being paid in credit or in scrip, and cheated in the annual "settling up" with landlord and merchants, the possibility of earning cash wages was in itself a major step toward economic freedom.

Responding to the cutoff of immigrant workers, some northern industries sent recruiting agents to the South as early as the spring of 1915. The United States Employment Service (USES), which was an agency of the federal government's Department of Labor, also played a role in recruiting southern blacks to work in northern industries, although by the summer of 1916, in response to southern white complaints, it had all but ceased such efforts. But by far the most influential single voice inspiring the African-American migration northwards was the widely-circulated black newspaper the *Chicago Defender*.

Robert Abbott, publisher of the *Chicago Defender*, came to be called the "Black Joshua." He was a propagandist as much as he was a journalist; in reporting on the Great Migration, the *Chicago Defender* was also helping to create it. Abbott's greatest publicity coup lay in his announcement/invention of "the Great Northern Drive." Early in 1917 the *Defender*, without a shred of supporting evidence, declared that on May 15, northern-bound passenger trains

Recently arrived in Chicago, these black men were being interviewed at the Chicago Urban League employment office. (Chicago Urban League Records, Special Collections, University Library, The University of Illinois at Chicago)

Migrants exiting a train in Chicago during the First World War (Chicago Urban League Records, Special Collections, University Library, The University of Illinois at Chicago)

would be leaving from stations all across the South, carrying away any and all blacks who wanted to leave, for a low fare. As portrayed in the *Defender*, the "Great Northern Drive" would be a replay of the biblical exodus: "Millions to Leave the South," a *Defender* headline proclaimed in January 1917, "Northern Invasion Will Start in Spring— Bound for the Promised Land."

There was, in fact, no organized plan for the mass transfer of the southern black population to the north and to freedom. In 1916 the Pennsylvania Railroad and the Illinois Central Railroad had issued a few thousand free passes to attract southern black laborers, which lent some credibility to Abbott's fable. But as the flamboyant publisher no doubt hoped, the wish served as father to the deed. Word of the

The Chicago Defender _____

The *Chicago Defender* was founded in 1905 by Robert Abbott. It was the largest-selling and most influential black newspaper in the United States in the years immediately before and after World War I.

Born in the South raised in Savannah, Georgia, and a graduate of Hampton Institute, Robert Sengstacke Abbott moved to Chicago in 1899 to practice law. He published the first issue of the *Defender* on May 5, 1905. Although a supporter of Booker T. Washington's educational philosophy, Abbott rejected Washington's policies of racial accommodationism. Abbott was a self-promoter and a showman (he billed his newspaper as the "World's Greatest Weekly"), and the *Defender* would make him one of Chicago's first black millionaires. But there is no doubt that Robert Abbott was genuinely committed to challenging racial inequality. He believed that his newspaper could be "one of the strongest weapons ever to be used in defense of a race." Poet Langston Hughes, who wrote for the *Defender*, called the newspaper the "voice of a voiceless people."

Under Abbott's influence, the *Defender* was outspoken in its condemnation of southern racism. Not since the abolitionist press in the years before the American Civil War had the South's racial crimes been so thoroughly chronicled—and unlike the abolitionist press, the *Defender*

"Great Northern Drive" spread through the South, was accepted as truth, and was embellished in the retelling. A *Chicago Defender* reader in Lutcher, Louisiana, wrote to the paper in May 1917 asking for advice on how to get a railroad pass to the North. In Lutcher alone he knew of "at least fifty men" who wanted to come north, if they could obtain free passes. He begged the editor to keep his letter confidential: "Please don't publish this because we have to whisper this around among our selves because the white folks are angry now because the negroes are going north."

was widely circulated and read in the South. Two-thirds of its circulation was outside Chicago, and by some estimates each copy was passed on to as many as 10 readers. Pullman porters, who regularly traveled the railroad routes between Chicago and the southern states, would drop bundles off along the way, and the papers were sold in black churches and barbershops to thousands of southern readers.

No southern-based black newspaper in the Jim Crow era could have gotten away with running the kinds of inflammatory stories and editorials that were a regular feature of the *Defender*. The newspaper publicized lynchings and other atrocities, often running blood-red headlines over such stories. The newspaper bitterly mocked the pretensions of southern chivalry: "White Gentleman Rapes Colored Girl," ran one famous headline. And the *Defender* advocated that blacks practice armed self-defense against racist violence. "WHEN THE MOB COMES," one headline proclaimed, "AND YOU MUST DIE, TAKE AT LEAST ONE WITH YOU."

In stark contrast to its grim reports from the South, the *Defender* promoted the glories of life in Chicago for African Americans, claiming that in the North blacks could expect respectful treatment from white merchants, integrated schools for their children, and genuine economic opportunity. The help-wanted classified ads in the paper were among its most popular feature.

During the war, the *Defender's* circulation climbed from 33,000 to 130,000. One observer reported that in Mississippi blacks "grab the *Defender* like a hungry mule grabs fodder." ◆

Many southern whites were indeed angered by talk of migration. They feared the loss of the cheap labor that for generations had made southern agriculture profitable, and they regarded the campaign by the *Defender* and others to encourage migration as an insult to the South's laws, social customs, and institutions. In some places, local authorites confiscated copies of the *Defender* from newsdealers. Some southern whites argued that "German agents," eager to stir up dissension and division in the southern states, were behind the whole effort.

In response, southern local and state governments passed laws to restrict or outlaw labor recruitment. Florida levied a fine of $1,000 on any person convicted of employing a black person to leave the state. One widely used legal device was the levying of exorbitant "licensing fees" for would-be northern industrial recruiters. The Macon, Georgia city council, for example, set the fee for recruiters in their city at $25,000, and required that before any northern recruiter be licensed he be vouched for by 10 local ministers, 10 manufacturers, and 25 local businessmen. When more than a thousand black passengers gathered at the Macon train station to board trains for Chicago in 1916, the police forcibly dispersed them. Northern-bound trains in Greenville, Mississippi were stopped by local authorities, and blacks found on board were dragged off the trains. At some train stations blacks seeking to purchase tickets to Chicago or other northern destinations were turned away by ticket sellers. Some emigrants made their trips in easy stages buying tickets for short distances north-ward, until they reached a train station where they were permitted to buy a ticket all the way to Chicago.

Some southern whites advocated a more conciliatory response: Perhaps the most degrading aspects of the Jim Crow system could be relaxed, perhaps wages could be gradually increased, certainly lynchings should come to an end. A white correspondent for the *Montgomery Advertiser* wrote in 1917:

"Wanted—10 molders. Must be experienced. $4.50 to $5.50 per day. Write B.F.R. Defender Office."

"3.60 per day can be made in a steel foundry in Minnesota, by strong, healthy, steady men. Open only to men living in Chicago. Apply in person, Chicago League on Urban Conditions Among Negroes, 3719 South State Street, Chicago, Illinois."

◆

—help-wanted ads during WWI, Chicago Defender

Why hunt for a cause [for black migration] when it's plain as the noonday sun the Negro is leaving this country for higher wages? He doesn't want to leave here but he knows if he stays here he will starve. . . . If the Negro race could get work of 50 cents per day he would stay here. He don't want to go. He is easily satisfied and will live on half rations and will never complain.

But the offer of "half rations" was too little and coming too late. The *Chicago Defender* mocked such efforts at discouraging northern migration:

Turn a deaf ear to everybody. . . . You see they are not lifting their laws to help you. Are they? Have they stopped their Jim Crow cars? Can you buy a Pullman sleeper where you wish? Will they give you a square deal in court yet? Once upon a time we permitted other people to think for us—today we are thinking and acting for ourselves with the result that our "friends" are getting alarmed at our progress. We'd like to oblige these unselfish (?) souls and remain slaves in the South, but to their section of the country we have said, as the song goes, "I hear you calling me," and have boarded the training singing, "Good-bye, Dixie land."

Not all southern blacks endorsed the "Great Northern Drive." Whites encouraged and in some instances financially rewarded black ministers, educators, and businessmen willing to encourage their race to remain in the South. Robert R. Moton, Booker T. Washington's successor at Tuskegee Institute, encouraged blacks to remain in the southern countryside, and carry out their patriotic duty to produce food during wartime. But such appeals generally fell on deaf ears. Ultimately neither the carrot nor the stick proved effective in stemming the tide of migrants, who even without the fabled free passes began to make their way north by the tens of thousands.

Emmett Scott, a longtime associate of Booker T. Washington, was one of the highest black appointees in the Wilson administration, serving as adviser on "Negro affairs" to the U.S. War Department. As part of his responsibilities, Scott kept close tabs on the mood of southern blacks during the war. In Scott's judgment it was the "United States mail [that] was about the most active and efficient labor agent" in attracting southern blacks to northern cities. Certainly the impact of letters, such as the one a Chicago carpenter sent to his family in Hattiesburg, Mississippi in the fall of 1917, must have been considerable:

> Mike, old boy, I was promoted on the first of the month. I was made first assistant to the head carpenter I should have been here 20 years ago. I just began to feel like a man. When he is out of place I take everything in charge and was raised to $95 per month. . . . My children are going to the same school with the whites and I don't have to umble to no one. I have registered, will vote the next election and there isn't any "yes sir" and "no sir"—its all yea and no and Sam and Bill."

Or consider another letter, written by a Chicago packinghouse worker to her sister that same year:

> I am well and thankful to say I am doing well. The weather and everything else was a surprise to me when I came. I got here in time to attend one of the greatest revivals in the history of my life—over 500 people joined the church. We had a Holy Ghost shower. You know I like to have run wild. It was snowing some nights and if you didnt hurry you could not get standing room. Please remember me kindly to any who ask of me. The people are rushing here by the thousands and I know if you come and rent a big house you can get all the roomers you want. You write me exactly when you are coming. . . . I can get a nice place for you to stop until

you can look around and see what you want. I am quite busy. I work in Swifts packing Co. in the sausage department. My daughter and I work for the same company—We get $1.50 a day and we pack so many sausages we dont have much time to play but it is a matter of a dollar with me and I feel that God made the path and I am walking therein. Tell your husband work is plentiful here and he wont have to loaf if he want to work.

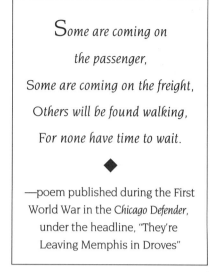

Some are coming on the passenger,

Some are coming on the freight,

Others will be found walking,

For none have time to wait.

◆

—poem published during the First World War in the *Chicago Defender*, under the headline, "They're Leaving Memphis in Droves"

Letters from the North were passed around and often read aloud in churches, barber shops, grocery stores, and other gathering places. Many of the migrants sent money home to their families, vivid proof of the economic opportunities in the North, and the means by which still more prospective migrants could afford to purchase railroad tickets. Unlike the experience of the 19th-century "Exodusters" and other earlier groups of black migrants who were so desperate to leave the South that they had little but blind faith to sustain them in the attempt to escape, those who undertook the Great Migration did so with a much greater degree of foreknowledge of what awaited them in the North. In Hattiesburg, Mississippi, the black community learned of opportunities in Chicago from the porters on the Gulf and Ship Island Railroad, which ran through their town. The miracles of life in the North came to dominate conversation. Mississippi blacks began to refer to the city familiarly as "Chi."

The Great Migration, among other things, represented a dramatic repudiation of Booker T. Washington's policies of racial accommodationism. Washington's influence had already begun to wane before his death in 1915. Southern blacks were no longer content to "cast down their buckets" where they were if doing so meant surrendering the dignity and rights of full American citizenship.

The Great Migration was not, of course, a political movement in any formal sense. There was no organization to join, no candidates to vote for, no party platform to uphold. The migration was the product of personal choices made by tens of thousands of individuals, each deciding on their own what would be best for them and their families. And yet, at the same time, the migration would never have taken place had there not been a large number of black people prepared to reject the lessons that southern society had tried to instill in them since birth. In that sense, the Great Migration did represent a kind of changing political consciousness, one with revolutionary implications for American society.

One of the best records of this shift in consciousness can be found in letters written to the editor of the *Chicago Defender* during the First World War. People wrote to the *Defender* for all kinds of reasons: to make inquiries and to ask for help, as well as to state their opinions. Taken together, what emerges from the letters is a kind of freedom manifesto and declaration of independence from the Jim Crow system. If the Great Migration represented a kind of revolution, it was a very American revolution. A Lexington, Mississippi schoolteacher wrote to the *Defender* in May 1917 to ask for help finding a northern employer. He complained that he was "compelled to teach 150 children without any assistance" for $27.00 a month, while a white schoolteacher in the same district received $100 a month for teaching only 30 students.

> I am so sick I am so tired of such conditions that I sometime think that life for me is not worth while and most eminently believe with Patrick Henry, "Give me liberty or give me death."

A New Orleans reader wrote that same month, "I indeed wish very much to come north anywhere in [Illinois]. will do since I am away from the Lynchman's noose and torchman's fire." Another reader from Dapne, Alabama wrote: "We are humane but we are not treated such we are treated like brute by our whites here we don't have no privilige no where in the south." A reader from Greenville, Mississippi wrote: "I want to get my famely out of this cursed south land down here a negro man is not as good as a white man's dog." A southern railroad cook wrote: "I am a man that would like to get work in some place where I can elevate my self & family & I think some where in the north is the place for me. . . ." A packinghouse worker from Alexandria, Louisiana wrote: "I has been here all my life but would be glad to go where I can educate my children where they can be of service to themselves, and this will never be here." A letter carrier from Augusta, Georgia wrote: "My children I wished to be educated in a different community than here. Where the school facilities are better and less prejudice shown and in fact where advantages are better for our people in all respect." And a laborer from Beaumont, Texas wrote: "I

Recent migrants awaiting job interviews outside Chicago Urban League office (Chicago Urban League Records, Special Collections, University Library, The University of Illinois at Chicago)

have been working for one company eight years and there is no advancement here for me and I would like to come where I can better my condition. . . ."

Equal rights, personal dignity, economic opportunity, the hope that one's children would enjoy a better life: such were the revolutionary demands of the Great Migration.

The letters to the *Chicago Defender* also provide a social portrait of some of those who made the journey North. Of course, the very act of writing a letter, which required a degree of literacy, however uncertain the spelling and grammar, excluded some people from the sample. The illiterate (and presumably the poorest) of the would-be migrants were not represented in the pages of the *Defender*. But those who could and did write came from a wide variety of social backgrounds. Some were sharecroppers from the countryside; many others had made their livings in southern cities. Some, like the schoolteacher from Lexington, Mississippi who cited Patrick Henry in his letter, were educated professionals. Others were skilled workers. "My dear sir," a man from Beaumont, Texas wrote to the editor in May 1917: "Please write me particulars concerning emigration to the north. I am a skilled machinist and longshoreman." Another letter that same month came from a man in Rome, Georgia: "I can Enamel, Grain & paint furniture. I can repair Violines, Guitars, & Mandolins, I am a first-class Umbrella Man. . . ." From Houston, Texas came this letter: "I am A masster firman I cand handle oil or I cand Burn Cole Keep up my pumps in Good order and i is A no. 1 masheane helper I cand doo moste en thange around the mill. . . ." From Atlanta, Georgia: "I am a glazer and want information on My line of work. I am a cutter and can do anything in a glazing room." From Brookhaven, Mississippi: "All I desire is a good position where I can earn a good liveing I am experienced in plumbing and all kinds of metal roofing and compositeon roofing. . . . Dont think that I am picking my Job as any position in any kind of shop would be appreciated have had

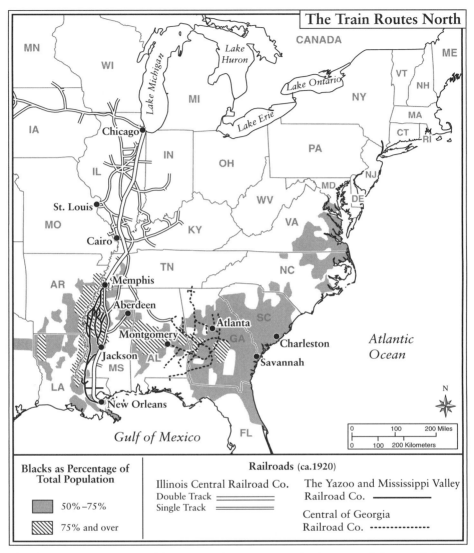

MN
WI
MI
Lake Michigan
Lake Huron
Lake Ontario
Lake Erie
CANADA
ME
VT
NH
NY
MA
IA
Chicago
IN
OH
PA
CT
RI
St. Louis
MO
Cairo
IL
KY
WV
VA
MD
DE
NJ
TN
NC
AR
Memphis
Aberdeen
Atlanta
SC
GA
Charleston
Montgomery
Jackson
MS
AL
Savannah
LA
New Orleans
Atlantic Ocean
N
Gulf of Mexico
FL

0   100   200 Miles
0   100   200 Kilometers

Blacks as Percentage of Total Population	Railroads (ca.1920)	
	Illinois Central Railroad Co.	The Yazoo and Mississippi Valley Railroad Co.
50%–75%	Double Track	
75% and over	Single Track	Central of Georgia Railroad Co.

The Illinois Central Railroad lines were the main routes leading out of the South for African Americans of the Great Migration.

12 years experience in pipe fitting." From Fullerton, Louisiana: "I am a railroad man by trade. . . . I have acted as yard master, anad manager of the switch engine and had charge of the local freight department. Please advise if you think I can secure a fairly good paying position up there. . . ."

Whether middle-class professionals, skilled workers, un-skilled laborers, or sharecroppers, what united the migrants was the aspiration for a better life. As one man wrote from Fayette, Georgia: "I am a college graduate and understand Bookkeeping. But I am not above doing hard work in a foundry or other industrial establishment."

So they boarded the trains in dusty southern towns and cities, laden down with suitcases or packages wrapped in paper, carrying with them as much of their earthly posses-sions as they hadn't already sold, or given away, or aban-doned. The trains pulled out of the station. At first nothing seemed different. After all, the migrants were confined to Jim Crow cars, which were dirty, crowded, and fitted with hard wooden seats. But once they crossed the Ohio River into the North, they could move and sit wherever they wanted, including next to white passengers if they so chose. Charles Denby, who had grown up on a cotton plantation in Lowndes County, Alabama, was one of those who made the journey, and never forgot the experience:

> We were hoping we'd get to see the Mason-Dixon line.
> I thought in my mind that it would look like a row of
> trees with some kind of white mark like the mark in the
> middle of the highway. We were hoping day would
> break before we got to the line. The train stopped in
> Covington, Kentucky just as the sun was rising. Some-
> one said the bridge ahead was the Mason-Dixon line.
> We were North. We didn't have to worry about sitting
> in the back, we felt good. . . . Hine and I met a boy from
> Columbus we had known in school. We agreed that if
> there was one white man on the train with a seat beside
> him, we'd sit there to see what he would do. All the
> things we'd heard before was like reading in the Bible.
> When I get to heaven I have milk and honey and pearly
> gates. I wanted to see was I there. We walked through
> the train feeling shaky. We thought any minute they
> would tell us to sit in the Negro coach. We found a seat

for two. Hines and the boy from Columbus sat down.
I continued to walk until I saw a seat by a white man. I
was very uncomfortable for the first hour. Hines seemed
very surprised that I continued to sit by the man. I
relaxed some. He was reading a paper and when he
finished half, he pushed it to me and asked if I wanted
to read. He wanted to know where I was going and said,
'Detroit is a nice place.' This was the most relaxing time
I had.

The Great Migration was a time of endings and beginnings. A poem, popular among southern blacks during the
war, was entitled, "Farewell! We're Good and Gone":

> It true we love de South all right,
> But, yes we loved God, too.
> An's when he comes ter help us out,
> What's left for us ter do?
> Den comes de North and wages high,
> Saying, come on up de horn,
> An' den you think we'll stay down here?
> 'Not us'—Good bye, we're gone. . . .

Like the slaves who escaped north on the underground
railroad in the 19th century, like the European immigrants
who disembarked at Ellis Island at the turn of the century,
those who took part in the Great Migration were determined
to win for themselves new opportunities and a new way of
life.

NOTES

p. 43 "Let us, while this war lasts . . ." W. E. B. DuBois quoted in David
Levering Lewis, *W. E. B. DuBois: Biography of a Race, 1868–1919* (New
York: Henry Holt and Company, 1993), p. 556.

p. 45 "Reading a article in the . . . *Chicago Defender* . . ." Quoted in Emmett J. Scott, ed., "Letters of Negro Migrants of 1916–1918," *Journal of Negro History*, 4 (July 1919), p. 294.

p. 48 "Please don't publish this . . ." Quoted in Emmet J. Scott, ed., "Additional Letters of Negro Migrants of 1916–1918," *Journal of Negro History*, 4 (October 1919), p. 417.

p. 51 "Why hunt for a cause . . ." Quoted in Chicago Commission on Race Relations, *The Negro in Chicago: A Study of Race Relations and a Race Riot* (Chicago: University of Illinois Press, 1922), p. 81.

p. 51 "Turn a deaf ear . . ." Quoted in St. Clair Drake and Horace R. Cayton, *Black Metropolis: A Study of Negro Life in a Northern City*, Vol I (New York: Harcourt, Brace and World, 1970), p. 59.

p. 52 "Mike, old boy . . ." Quoted in Scott, "Additional Letters of Negro Migrants of 1916–1918," p. 459.

p. 52 "I am well and thankful . . ." Quoted in Scott, "Additional Letters of Negro Migrants of 1916–1918," p. 457.

p. 54 "I am so sick I am so tired . . ." Quoted in Scott, "Letters of Negro Migrants of 1916–1918," p. 304.

p. 54 "I indeed wish very much to come north . . ." Quoted in Scott, "Additional Letters of Negro Migrants of 1916–1918," p. 450.

p. 55 "We are humane but we are not treated such . . ." Quoted in Scott, "Additional Letters of Negro Migrants of 1916–1918," p. 452.

p. 55 "I want to get my famely out of this cursed south . . ." Quoted in Scott, "Additional Letters of Negro Migrants of 1916–1918," p. 452.

p. 55 "I am a man that would like to get work . . ." Quoted in Scott, "Letters of Negro Migrants of 1916–1918," p. 306.

p. 55 "I has been here all my life . . ." Quoted in Scott, "Additional Letters of Negro Migrants of 1916–1918," p. 434.

p. 55 "My children I wished to be educated . . ." Quoted in Scott, "Additional Letters of Negro Migrants of 1916–1918," p. 437.

pp. 55–56 "I have been working for one company . . ." Quoted in Scott, "Letters of Negro Migrants of 1916–1918," p. 314.

p. 56 "My dear sir . . ." Quoted in Scott, "Letters of Negro Migrants of 1916–1918," p. 293.

p. 56 "I can Enamel, Grain & paint furniture . . ." Quoted in Scott, "Letters of Negro Migrants of 1916–1918," p. 299.

p. 56 "I am A masster firman . . ." Quoted in Scott, "Letters of Negro Migrants of 1916–1918," p. 299.

p. 56 "I am a glazer . . ." Quoted in Scott, "Letters of Negro Migrants of 1916–1918," p. 300.

p. 56 "All I desire is a good position . . ." Quoted in Scott, "Letters of Negro Migrants of 1916–1918," p. 300.

p. 57 "I am a railroad man by trade . . ." Quoted in Scott, "Letters of Negro Migrants of 1916–1918," p. 335.

p. 58 "I am a college graduate . . ." Quoted in Scott, "Letters of Negro Migrants of 1916–1918," p. 302.

p. 58 "We were hoping we'd get to see . . ." Charles Denby, *Indignant Heart: A Black Worker's Journal* (Boston: South End Press, 1980), p. 27.

p. 59 "It true we love de South all right, . . ." Quoted in Carole Marks, *Farewell—We're Good and Gone* (Bloomington: Indiana University Press, 1989), p. v.

5

"You Notice There Ain't No Jim Crow . . .": Life in the North, 1916–1920

The trains rolled northward, day after day, in 1916, 1917, 1918, 1919, and on into the next decade. And day after day, year after year, thousands of African-American migrants from all across the South stepped out for the first time onto train platforms in New York, Pennsylvania, Illinois, and Michigan to begin new lives. They felt tired from the long trip, disoriented, apprehensive, and hopeful, all in about equal measure, as they took their first

The Urban League helped migrant families like this one find housing and employment. (Chicago Woman's Aid Records, Special Collections, University Library, The University of Illinois at Chicago)

steps into this strange, new promised land of the North. They encountered noise, and confusion, and crowds unlike anything they had ever seen before.

Sometimes they were lucky enough to be met at the station by family or friends who had already made the journey north. In some cities, earlier arrivals formed self-help groups, like the Mississippi Club in Chicago, that met the incoming trains and helped migrants find their way around in the first few confusing days of their move. The Detroit chapter of the national Urban League met many of the trains coming into their city and helped orient the newcomers. Many times, however, the new arrivals were on their own. When a young New Orleans musician named Louis Armstrong arrived at the Illinois Central railroad station in Chicago, he was unable to find the friend who was supposed to meet him there: "I saw a million people," he later recalled, "but not Mister Joe, and I didn't give a damn who else was there. I never seen a city that big. All those tall buildings. I thought they were universities. I said, no, this is the wrong city. I was fixing to take the next train back home. . . ."

But if family and friends failed to meet them, most of the new arrivals knew enough about the city to which they had come to know that there was a place nearby where they could find people like themselves. Those like Louis Armstrong who got off the train at the Illinois Central terminal in Chicago could ask a fellow passenger, or a policeman, or a passerby how to get to the South Side, an area of the city that became known as "Bronzeville" for the skin color of most of its newest residents. Those who got off the train in Detroit could ask how to get to the city's East Side, then becoming known as the "East Side Colored District." In New York it was Harlem, in Boston it was Roxbury. It was always someplace where many blacks already lived. One thing moving to the Promised Land did not mean, for the overwhelming majority of the migrants, was moving into a white neighborhood.

Just which urban black community in the North the migrants moved to had a lot to do with where an individual had started his or her journey northward. Migratory routes almost always ran due north, mirroring the paths followed by the major north-south railroad lines. Those who had grown up in states bordering the Atlantic, such as Florida, Georgia, the Carolinas, or Virginia usually wound up settling in New York, Pennsylvania, Connecticut, Massachusetts, or New Jersey. Those who had grown up in Mississippi, Alabama, Arkansas, Louisiana, and Texas moved to or at least passed through Chicago. (Many who got off the train in the Illinois Central station would soon reboard other trains for cities in bordering states like Indiana, Michigan, and Ohio.) Because of this pattern, regional cultures, kinship ties, and personal bonds formed in the South remained strong in the North for the first generation of the Great Migration.

The Great Migration represented two dramatic changes in the demographic profile of black America: African Americans were becoming a people of the North as well as the South—and they were becoming an urban as well as a rural people. In 1910, according to the U.S. Census, over 72 percent of blacks lived in rural communities, under 28 percent in urban communities. Ten years later, the percent of blacks in rural communities had declined to 66 percent, and the percent living in urban communities had climbed to 34, over a third. When blacks moved north, they moved to cities, and not only that, but they tended to move to the largest cities available. According to the 1920 U.S. Census, 60 percent of Illinois' black population lived in Chicago; 68 percent of Michigan's black population lived in Detroit; and 75 percent of New York State's black population lived in New York City. Some smaller cities in the North also experienced significant if lesser increases in their black population, including Albany, Poughkeepsie, and Buffalo in New York; Newark, Trenton, and Jersey City in New Jersey; Columbus, Cincinnati, Akron, and Youngstown in Ohio; Gary and Indianapolis in Indiana; Hartford in Connecticut; and Holyoke in Massachusetts.

Centers of African-American Urban Population, 1920	
New York City	160,585
Philadelphia	135,599
Chicago	112,536
Washington, D.C.	110,711
Baltimore	108,696
New Orleans	101,303
St. Louis	70,282
Birmingham	70,256
Atlanta	62,880
Memphis	61,238
	Source: U.S. Census data, 1920

In absolute numbers, New York City received the greatest number of African-American migrants in the first decade of the Great Migration, with its black population growing from 91,709 in 1910 to 152,467 in 1920, an increase of over 66 percent. By the latter year, they made up just under 3 percent of the city's 5,620,000 inhabitants. New York City displaced Washington, D.C. as the largest center of black population in the nation. In terms of percentage, Detroit was the city that was affected the most by the Great Migration; its black population increased from 5,741 in 1910 to 40,838 in 1920, an increase of over 600 percent. In 1920 blacks made up just over 4 percent of Detroit's 993,000 inhabitants. Other cities experienced large relative and absolute growth in their black populations. But it was Chicago, more than any other city, that came to symbolize the Great Migration. "You could not rest in your bed at night for Chicago," recalled one Mississippi black who would soon join the northward trek. Perhaps, this was because of the highly visible role played by the *Chicago Defender* in promoting the Great Migration; perhaps it was due to the city's role as transportation hub for the entire Midwest; perhaps it was the ready availability of jobs for unskilled labor in the city's stockyards, mills, and mail-order houses; perhaps it was the sheer concentration of economic enterprise, political savvy, and cultural vibrancy that could be found in the city's black community by the closing days of the First World War. For whatever reason, more than any other northern city, Chicago served as a good illustration of both the potential and limitations of this new "promised land."

Chicago was an exciting place to be during the First World War, whether one was black or white. There were jobs to be had for the asking, and if the rising cost of living ate up a good portion of a factory or stockyard worker's wages, there was still likely to be some money left over to spend on new clothes, furniture for the apartment, an ice cream cone for a child, a night out at a restaurant or a movie for parents, and maybe even the down payment for a house. Everywhere there was a sense of movement, new faces, a city on the make. In downtown Chicago, the "crowds surge, weaving currents along the sidewalks," wrote a reporter for the *New Republic* during the war. "Street-cars, motors, trucks, wagons, congest the street. There is the continuous roar of action; the life-blood of the city pulsates in its great arteries; a static sense of energy is in the air."

Chicago's black population increased from 44,103 in 1910 to 109,458 in 1920, an increase of nearly 150 percent, leaping from 10th to 3rd place on the list of the 10 greatest centers of African-American population in the United States. The U.S. Census Bureau estimated that nine-tenths of the jump in the city's black population was due to immigration rather than natural increase. In 1910 blacks had accounted for 2 percent of the city's total population; by 1920 they accounted for over 4 percent of the city's nearly 3 million inhabitants. Of course, that meant that they were still only a small proportion of the city's population. Chicago was still overwhelmingly a city of European immigrants, with residents of German, Polish, Jewish, Hungarian, Lithuanian, Greek, Italian, and of course Irish stock all well represented. In 1920 72 percent of the city consisted of immigrants or their children. But European immigrants, and especially their children, tended to resemble one another. Not so the new wave of migrants from the American South. Because of skin color and discriminatory housing patterns, they were a highly visible component. By 1920, 90 percent of Chicago's African-American population was concentrated into one majority black district, the old South Side, the district stretching from Twelfth to Thirty-first Streets and from Wentworth to Wabash Avenues. The corner of Thirty-first and State Streets was thought of as the center of black Chicago, since it was there that many black business and professional men maintained offices. Smaller, less intensely segregated colonies of black residents were also emerging in the Woodlawn

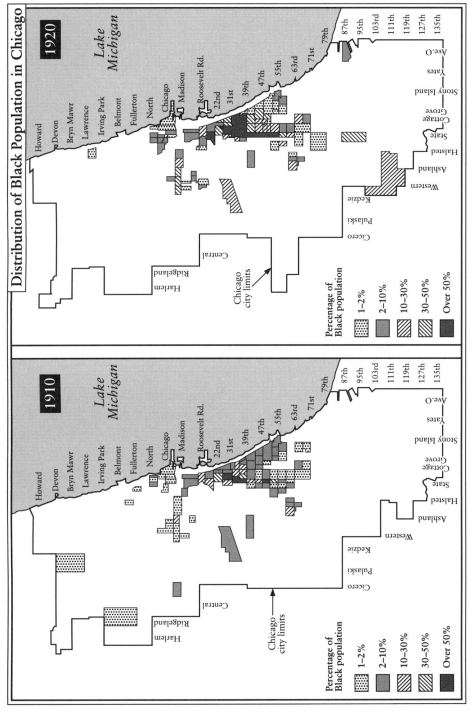

Distribution of Black Population in Chicago

1920

Lake Michigan

Howard
Devon
Bryn Mawr
Lawrence
Irving Park
Belmont
Fullerton
North
Chicago
Madison
Roosevelt Rd.
22nd
31st
39th
47th
55th
63rd
71st
79th
87th
95th
103rd
111th
119th
127th
135th

Harlem
Ridgeland
Central
Cicero
Pulaski
Kedzie
Western
Ashland
Halsted
State
Cottage Grove
Stony Island
Yates
Ave. O

Chicago city limits

Percentage of Black population
1–2%
2–10%
10–30%
30–50%
Over 50%

1910

Lake Michigan

Howard
Devon
Bryn Mawr
Lawrence
Irving Park
Belmont
Fullerton
North
Chicago
Madison
Roosevelt Rd.
22nd
31st
39th
47th
55th
63rd
71st
79th
87th
95th
103rd
111th
119th
127th
135th

Harlem
Ridgeland
Central
Cicero
Pulaski
Kedzie
Western
Ashland
Halsted
State
Cottage Grove
Stony Island
Yates
Ave. O

Chicago city limits

Percentage of Black population
1–2%
2–10%
10–30%
30–50%
Over 50%

In 1910 African Americans made up 2 percent of Chicago's population; in 1920 this was double at 4 percent of 3 million inhabitants.

neighborhood; on the West Side in the area bounded by Lake Street, Ashland, Austin, and Warren Avenues; and on the North Side.

Chicago's black "Old Settlers" felt distinctly ambivalent about the newcomers crowding into the city's black belt. On the one hand, the position of the entire black community within the city, whether long-established or recently arrived, would clearly be strengthened by the arrival of reinforcements from the South. There would be more patronage for black-owned businesses and black professionals. By 1920, blacks in Chicago owned, among 1,200 other businesses, 2 banks, 12 bakeries, 211 barbershops, 8 clothing stores, 31 drug stores, 7 ice cream shops, 52 real estate offices, 87 restaurants, and 21 undertaking establishments. Chicago had 109 black physicians in 1910 and 195 in 1920, while the number of black lawyers more than doubled, from 44 to 95. These were among the fruits of the Great Migration. The "Stroll" along South State Street, which took one past numerous thriving black-owned businesses, was a monument to black economic enterprise. As Langston Hughes remembered from his first visit to the city in 1918, "South State Street was in its glory . . . a teeming Negro street with crowded theaters, restaurants, and cabarets."

The urban black churches also gained thousands of new members as a result of the Great Migration. The membership of the prestigious Olivet Baptist Church, located on South Dearborn Street in Chicago, jumped by more than 5,000 from 1916 to 1919. By the start of the 1920s Olivet had over 9,000 members, which made it the largest Protestant church in the United States. Many of the migrants also formed new churches. Some of the new churches were housed in impressive buildings; others were run out of storefronts. Religion was both a unifying and divisive force within the urban black community. Churches offered their parishioners an elaborate range of social, cultural, and practical activities and services, as well as tending to their spiritual needs. But

The Great Migration made Olivet Baptist Church in Chicago the largest Protestant congregation in the United States. (Chicago Commission on Race Relations, *The Negro in Chicago,* 1920, p. 140)

African-American parishioners were stratified by religious preference. Longer-established and financially better-off blacks tended to be Methodists and Episcopalians; the majority of newcomers were Baptists; and those at the bottom of the social scale gravitated towards revivalist, Pentecostalist, and spiritualist cults.

The Great Migration also meant more voters showing up on election day in the black community, which meant more clout with the city's ruling white politicians, and more possibilities for blacks to hold office. Already in 1915 black Chicago had elected its first black alderman, Oscar DePriest, as well as making a significant contribution to the election of the new Republican mayor William ("Big Bill") Hale Thompson. DePriest would remain a political power broker in the city for decades, and he would later go on to become the first black elected to the U.S. Congress since the end of Reconstruction. By 1919 Carl Sandburg, then a reporter for a Chicago newspaper, described Chicago's black belt as "probably the strongest effective unit of political power, good or bad, in America," which was quite a compliment in a city known for the effectiveness of its political machines.

On the other hand, Chicago's black elite, proud of their hard-won achievements including neat residential neighborhoods, sturdy churches, solid educations, and polished manners, viewed the presence of the often rough and rowdy newcomers with considerable and understandable apprehension. Would the arrival of so many migrants from the Deep South only serve to confirm the racial stereotyping that the black Old Settlers had worked so hard to undermine? Too many whites already believed that blacks brought with them an epidemic of vice, crime, disorder, and declining property values. So the migrants were bombarded with advice, some of it helpful, some of it merely patronizing. The Chicago chapter of the Urban League passed out cards to newcomers with a list of "self-help" rules that betrayed a preoccupation with preserving the appearance of respectability.

If You are a Stranger in the City

If you want a job   If you want a place to live
If you are having trouble with your employer
If you want information or advice of any kind

CALL UPON

The CHICAGO LEAGUE ON URBAN
CONDITIONS AMONG NEGROES

3719 South State Street

Telephone Douglas 9098   T. ARNOLD HILL, Executive Secretary

No charges—no fees. We want to help YOU

*This wallet-sized card was distributed to migrants by the Chicago Urban League.
Top: front of card, bottom: back of card.* (Aldis Family Papers, Special Collection University Library, The University of Illinois at Chicago)

SELF-HELP

1. Do not loaf. Get a job at once.
2. Do not live in crowded rooms. Others can be obtained.
3. Do not carry on loud conversations in street cars and public places.
4. Do not keep your children out of school.
5. Do not send for your family until you get a job.
6. Do not think you can hold your job unless you are industrious, sober, efficient and prompt.

   Cleanliness and fresh air are necessary for good health. In case of sickness send immediately for a good physician. Become an active member in some church as soon as you reach the city.

Issued by

Even the militant *Chicago Defender* advised newcomers to avoid the use of "vile language" in public places, and to discard the identifying marks of their southern origins, describing the wearing of overalls or head rags, for instance, as a "mark of servitude."

Some of the advice offered by the Urban League, like the suggestion "Get a job at once," proved practical. There were jobs to be had in wartime Chicago, and good ones.

As African Americans became a northern and an urban people, they also began to find a footing in industrial America. One of the main activities of the Chicago chapter of the Urban League was acting as an employment referral service. In 1918, the Urban League helped nearly 7,000 black migrants find jobs in the city; the following year they found places for over 12,000.

One of the most striking figures recorded in the 1920 U.S. Census was the overall decline in the number of gainfully employed African-American workers over the age of 10. In 1910 the census had counted 5,192,535 employed workers; in 1920 it counted only 4,824,151. Since the black population had increased in the meantime, that suggests the absence

Gainfully Occupied African-American Population in the United States in 1920*		
Industry	Number	Percentage
Agriculture, forestry, etc.	2,178,888	45.2
Domestic and personal service	1,064,590	22
Manufacturing and mechanical industries	886,810	18.4
Transportation	312,421	6.4
Trade	140,467	3
Professional service	80,183	1.7
Public service	50,552	1
Others	110,240	2.3
Total United States	4,824,151	
* Ten years of age and older	Source: U.S. Census data, 1920	

of some group of workers previously included. The most obvious candidate is child labor in southern cotton fields. As black families moved north, they were much more likely to have their 10, 11, and 12-year-old children enrolled in school, rather than laboring at home. The number of workers employed in agriculture, forestry, and animal husbandry dropped in absolute numbers from 2,893,674 in 1910 to 2,178,888 in 1920, and as a percentage of the total black work force from 55.7 percent in 1910 to 45.2 percent 10 years later. The number involved in "manufacturing and mechanical pursuits" increased in the same period from 12.6 percent in 1910 to 18.4 percent. This gain in industrial occupations primarily involved black men; while some black women found employment in factories and packinghouses, the overwhelming majority of them continued to work in "domestic and personal service." In Chicago in 1920 this category included 63.8 percent of all black women workers. Black women who did find industrial employment during the years of wartime scarcity were the first to be laid off after the war when demand for labor slackened. And of the black women remaining in manufacturing by 1920, many worked in industries closely related to domestic service, such as laundries.

A detailed survey of black employment in Chicago in 1920 showed that the stockyards were the city's largest employers of black labor. Swift employed 2,278 blacks at the time of the survey, Armour an additional 2,084, and the Morris & Co. stockyards 1,400. International Harvester, a manufacturer of agricultural machinery, employed 1,551 blacks that year. And 1,423 blacks were employed by the Sears, Roebuck & Co. mail-order house.

Despite their increased employment opportunities in manufacturing, most black males were still restricted to unskilled labor, notwithstanding the fact that in the South they had often worked in skilled crafts. In meat packing-houses blacks worked on the killing floor, where they killed the cattle and pigs and cleaned up the resulting mess. In steel foundries they fed coal into the blast furnaces, the hottest and often most lethal job available in the industry.

If conditions for blacks in manufacturing were to change, they were going to need the backing of organized labor. And during the war, after years of indifference or hostility to black workers, the trade union movement, or at least sections of it, began to take notice of the tens of thousands of black migrants pouring into northern cities. Many of the unions affiliated with the American Federation of Labor (AFL) retained whites-only membership clauses or achieved the same ends through more informal practices. The northern building trades were notoriously lily white and would remain so for decades to come. Other unions proved equally recalcitrant. The International Association of Machinists, for example, did not have a single black member in Chicago in 1920 (and, in fact, its constitution would forbid the enrollment of black members until 1948); while the Electrician's Union had a total of one black among its 11,000 Chicago members. Many white workers remained fearful of blacks as economic competitors, particularly as the war-induced labor scarcity came to an end, while many blacks remained suspicious of union intentions.

But the newer industrial unions proved more welcoming to black workers. The International Ladies Garment Workers Union (ILGWU), under socialist leadership, was exceptionally sympathetic; when employers tried to break a

> *W*ell, son, I'll tell you:
>
> Life for me ain't been no
>
> crystal stair.
>
> It's had tacks in it,
>
> And splinters,
>
> And boards torn up,
>
> And places with no carpet
>
> on the floor—
>
> Bare.
>
> But all the time
>
> I'se been a-climbin' on,
>
> And reachin' landin's
>
> And turnin' corners . . .
>
> ◆
>
> —"Mother to Son,"
> Langston Hughes, 1922

garment workers strike in Chicago in 1917 by the tried-and-true method of hiring black strikebreakers, the ILGWU responded by admitting all the black workers as full and equal members of the union. By 1920 the Chicago local of the ILGWU had 450 black members. In the stockyards, the unions recognized that they would never be able to make any solid gains as long as the employers could manipulate racial hostilities and divide the work force, as they had so successfully done back in 1904. So in its organizing drives in 1917–18, the Stockyard Labor Council made a concerted effort to reach out to black workers, and as a result secured an eight-hour day and increased wages for its members. Not that racial harmony was achieved, by any means. In the early summer of 1919, a wave of unauthorized strikes in the stockyards pitted white union members against black non-members. But the stockyard unions kept trying to win over black workers to their side. On July 6, 1919, in a renewed organizing drive, the Amalgamated Meat Cutters and Butcher Workmen of North America (AMCBW) sponsored a parade of black union members that wound its way through Chicago's black belt and ended in an open air rally near the stockyards. There they were joined by a separate column of white marchers who had come along a different route. At the rally a black AMCBW organizer told the crowd, now composed about equally of black and white workers:

> You notice there ain't no Jim Crow cars here today. That's what organization does. The truth is there ain't no Negro problem any more than there's an Irish problem or a Russian or a Polish or a Jewish or any other problem. There is only the human problem, that's all. All we demand is the open door. You give us that, and we won't ask nothin' more of you.

One measure of the growing sympathy for the union cause in the black community was the shift in the *Chicago De-*

fender's editorial line. At the start of the Great Migration, the *Defender* had cautioned blacks against what it saw as the hypocritical promises of trade union organizers; by 1919, however, the newspaper was calling on black workers to join unions whenever they could.

If the first commandment of the Chicago Urban League's advice to newcomers—"Get a job at once."—was realistic in the war years, the second one—"Do not live in crowded rooms. Others can be obtained."—unfortunately bordered on pure fantasy. Where were the migrants supposed to go? While the boundaries of the black belt on Chicago's South Side expanded during the war, the density of population increased far more dramatically. In December 1916 the Chicago *Daily News* reported on the difficulties faced by the black migrants in obtaining decent housing. The report quoted a "prominent real estate dealer" who observed:

> Chicago's colored population is growing with great rapidity and its welfare cannot be ignored. A civic policy which holds that anything is good enough and nothing is too bad to be permitted in a colored residence or business district is now in force. The better class of colored persons will move away from such districts, leaving an element which discredits the race and creating a plague spot endangering the physical and moral health of the entire city.

In the same article, the *Daily News* reporter informed readers of what he had found in a survey of every house in a three-block district of the South Side:

> Many of the building did not have lights in the hallways. One did not have any back porches, and the dark hallways were full of clotheslines and freshly washed clothes. Few had bathrooms, and in many there was no plumbing or else the water was shut off on account of non-payment of rent. Rickety stairways without hand-

rails, gaping rents in the plaster, leaky roofs, wet basements, indiscriminate refuse and dirt and other violations of health and building regulations of the city abounded.

In this district were 1,406 colored persons and not more than twenty-five white persons. Only one piece of property, however, was owned by a colored man.

What the *Daily News* failed to mention were the policies adopted by many white property owners, landlords, real estate agents, and community associations that deliberately enforced de facto residential segregation in Chicago, preventing the poorer inhabitants of the South Side from seeking better housing. "Restrictive covenants" were routinely written into the deeds of houses in many white neighborhoods, legally forbidding their sale to any nonwhite buyer (it would only be in 1948 that the U.S. Supreme Court in *Shelley* v. *Kraemer* ruled that restrictive covenants violated the equal protection clauses of the Constitution). Landlords and real estate agents could charge black tenants and home buyers more money for dilapidated housing, knowing they could not readily move elsewhere. Rents in the black belt ordinarily ran 25 percent more for housing than in comparable white areas. Landlords had little financial incentive to maintain apartments properly, knowing that they could find tenants regardless of the condition of their property. They could subdivide what were intended to be single-family homes into tiny,

The antidote to persecution . . . is power, and if the northern Negroes are more numerous and more urgently needed in our industrial life, they could protect themselves from the worst forms of discrimination . . . Thus the Negro, a half century after emancipation, is to-day entering upon a new stage in his progress "up from slavery."

◆

—editorial, *The New Republic*, July 1, 1916

wretched apartments, and thus squeeze even more profits out of a building.

In border districts of the city, where black tenants and home buyers began making inroads into formerly all-white neighborhoods, organized groups of white property owners sprang up in opposition. Feelings ran particularly high in Hyde Park, a neighborhood below the "Old South Side"; here white residents had organized it to keep out blacks as early as 1908. They used a variety of tactics, boycotting merchants who sold goods to black customers, and calling on white employers to discharge any black employees who crossed the residential racial divide. The *Property Owners Journal* published by the Kenwood (the area directly above Hyde Park and below the Old South Side, running from Fifty-third to Forty-seventh Streets) and Hyde Park Property Owners' Association, representing a thousand white property owners in this increasingly contested district, declared in its January 1, 1920 issue:

> Every colored man who moves into Hyde Park knows that he is damaging his white neighbors' property. Therefore, he is making war on the white man. Consequently, he is not entitled to any consideration and forfeits his right to be employed by a white man. If employers should adopt a rule of refusing to employ Negroes who persist in residing in Hyde Park to the damage of the white man's property, it would soon show good results.
>
> The Negro is using the Constitution and its legal rights to abuse the moral rights of the white.

Racial tensions, in Chicago and elsewhere, were heightened by the emotional intensity of wartime. To mobilize public opinion behind the war effort, the Wilson administration unleashed a barrage of propaganda intended to make Americans hate the enemy—and to hate any fellow

The Silent Parade of the NAACP *protesting racial violence,* 1917 (Special Collections and Archives, W. E. B. DuBois Library, University of Massachusetts, Amherst)

Americans who might be perceived of as insufficiently patriotic. New laws were passed making criticism of the war a federal crime. German Americans found themselves shunned and sometimes physically abused by mobs; socialist and pacifist opponents of the war were attacked in the streets and indicted in the courts. Vigilante groups attacked and sometimes murdered radical labor organizers.

And the emotions spilled over onto blacks as well. In July 1917, in two days of terrible bloodletting, rampaging white mobs massacred dozens—some maintained hundreds—of blacks in East St. Louis, Illinois. Three square blocks of houses in the black community were burned to the ground, some with their tenants trapped inside. Eight thousand Harlem residents, the men dressed in black, the women and children in white, marched in protest down Fifth Avenue to

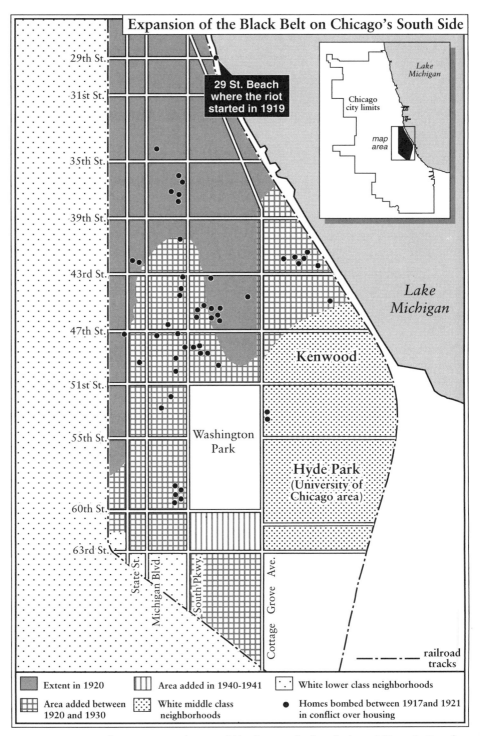

Expansion of the Black Belt on Chicago's South Side

29th St.

31st St.

29 St. Beach
where the riot
started in 1919

35th St.

39th St.

43rd St.

47th St.

Kenwood

Lake
Michigan

51st St.

55th St.

Washington
Park

Hyde Park
(University of
Chicago area)

60th St.

63rd St.

State St.

Michigan Blvd.

South Pkwy.

Cottage Grove Ave.

railroad
tracks

Lake
Michigan

Chicago
city limits

map
area

Extent in 1920	Area added in 1940-1941	White lower class neighborhoods
Area added between 1920 and 1930	White middle class neighborhoods	Homes bombed between 1917 and 1921 in conflict over housing

Between 1917 and 1921 many homes of blacks were firebombed on Chicago's South
Side as whites attempted to keep blacks from moving into their neighborhoods.

The Chicago Race Riot _____

The incident that sparked the Chicago riot took place around four o'clock on the steamy Sunday afternoon of July 27, 1919, when a 17-year-old black youth named Eugene Williams unwittingly crossed the invisible line in the water dividing white and black bathers along Chicago's Twenty-ninth Street beach. There had already been trouble on shore that afternoon between groups of white and black bathers: skirmishing with rocks and curses for space along the waterfront. Williams, caught offshore, was kept from returning to the beach by stone-throwing. One stone struck him in the forehead, and finally exhausted, he drowned. A white police officer refused to arrest the white man whom blacks on the beach believed had thrown the fatal stone. Rumors spread up and down the beach, and back into residential communities on the South Side. Whites believed that it was a white swimmer who had been killed by a rock thrown by blacks; blacks believed that white police had actually stood by idly while whites pelted Williams with stones.

An angry, racially mixed crowd gathered. A black man was arrested by police for disorderly conduct. And then another black man pulled out a pistol and fired at the police, and was in turn shot and killed by a black policeman. The riot was on. Fighting soon spread from the beach in neighboring districts of the city. Over the next few days whites and blacks caught in the "wrong" part of the city, many of them while traveling on streetcars to and from work, were killed by angry mobs. Most of the violence was confined to the South Side of the city, with isolated incidents in the downtown "Loop." White newspapers like the Chicago *Daily News* and black newspapers like the *Chicago Defender* inflamed the situation by printing false accounts of mob attacks against women and children; one headline in the *Daily News* on July 29 read "Attack White Women as Race Riots Grow," while the *Defender* reported on August 2 that a black woman and her three-month-old baby had been killed by white rioters. Neither story had any basis in fact.

The police were unable to contain the violence as the death toll mounted, until finally on the fourth day Mayor Thompson summoned the Illinois militia to restore peace. Many black veterans of the Eighth

These two photographs record the death of a black man pursued and stoned by a white mob in the Chicago race riot, July 1919. (from Chicago Commission on Race Relations, The Negro in Chicago, 1920, p. 12)

Regiment of the Illinois National Guard, recently disbanded after service in the war, donned their uniforms and offered their services to the militia and police to help restore order. The Chicago Federation of Labor distributed an article to its members calling on them to "protect colored fellow-workers from the unreasoning frenzy of race prejudice" (there was, in fact, relatively little violence between white and black workers in the stockyards and mills during the rioting, but this probably had more to do with the fact that many black workers stayed off the job that week to avoid trouble than any class solidarity of black and white workers). With the appearance of the militia, and a providential change in weather that brought two days of rain, the rioting finally ended. The total casualties of six days of intermittent race warfare in the city was 23 blacks and 15 whites left dead, 342 blacks and 176 whites injured, and a thousand people left homeless.

One of the distinctive features of the Chicago riot was the combativeness of both races. In East St. Louis in 1917, the violence had been largely one-sided, with white mobs mutilating and murdering hapless and unresisting black victims. In Chicago in 1919, blacks fought back and even initiated violence against whites. Walter F. White, an NAACP official, attributed the difference to the role that black soldiers played in the recent "war to end all wars":

> Finally, the new spirit aroused in Negroes by their war experiences enters into the problem. From Local [Draft] Board No. 4, embracing the neighborhood in the vicinity of State and 35th Streets, containing over 30,000 inhabitants of which fully ninety per cent are colored, over 9,000 men registered and 1,850 went to [military training] camp. These men, with their new outlook on life injected the same spirit of independence into their companions, a thing that is true of many other sections of America. One of the greater surprises to many of those who came down to "'clean out the niggers" is that the same "niggers" fought back. Colored men saw their own kind being killed, heard of many more and believed that their lives and liberty were at stake. In such a spirit most of the fighting was done.

In the aftermath of the rioting, Illinois governor Frank Lowden appointed a blue-ribbon group, the Chicago Commission on Race Relations, to investigate the causes of the rioting. Its membership was drawn half from the white community and half from the black community, and included *Chicago Defender* publisher Robert Abbott. The commission's conclusion, delivered in its 1922 report, *The Negro in Chicago*, was "that the relation of whites and Negroes in the United States is our most grave and perplexing domestic problem." ◆

the beat of muffled drums in a protest organized by the NAACP, carrying signs with slogans like "Mr. President, Why Not Make America Safe for Democracy?"

In Chicago, tensions over jobs and housing led to thousands of small scale, mostly unrecorded confrontations between whites and blacks during the war. Langston Hughes, visiting Chicago while still a high school student in the summer of 1918, wandered by chance into a Polish neighborhood where he was surrounded by a gang of young men. "We don't 'low no niggers in this street," they taunted him, knocking him to the ground with a blow to the jaw, then chasing him away in a shower of stones. Between 1917 and 1919, two dozen houses in Chicago owned or occupied by blacks were bombed by whites seeking to drive them out of the neighborhood. The worst violence came in the "Red Summer" of 1919 (so named for the blood spilled during it). Twenty-five cities erupted in race riots that summer, including outbreaks in Charleston, South Carolina; Washington, D.C.; and Omaha, Nebraska. And the worst riot of all took place in Chicago.

Chicago and other northern cities had not turned out to be the "Promised Land" after all. Was the Great Migration a mistake? In the aftermath of the Red Summer of 1919, a number of black leaders asked themselves that question. In January 1920, W. E. B. DuBois wrote in the NAACP's journal *The Crisis*:

The migration of Negroes from South to North continues and ought to continue. The North is no paradise—as East St. Louis, Washington, Chicago, and Omaha prove; but the South is at best a system of caste and insult and at worst a Hell. With ghastly and persistent regularity, the lynching of Negroes in the South continues—every year, every month, every day; wholesale murders and riots have taken place at Norfolk, Longview, Arkansas, Knoxville, and 24 other places in a single year. The outbreaks in the North have been fiercer, but they have quickly been curbed; no attempt has been made to saddle the whole blame on Negroes; and the cities where riots have taken place are today safer and better for Negroes than ever before. . . . We can vote in the North. We can hold office in the North. As workers in northern establishments, we are getting good wages, decent treatment, healthful homes and schools for our children. Can we hesitate? COME NORTH!

Ordinary black citizens seemed to agree. The Chicago Commission on Race Relations did a detailed survey in 1920 of the experience of black migrants to the city. As recorded in *The Negro in Chicago*, answers to the question "Do you get more comfort and pleasure from your higher wages?" included:

1. Yes. Living in better houses, can go into almost any place if you have money, and then the schools are so much better here.
2. Yes, I live better, save more, and feel more like a man.
3. Yes, I can buy more. My wife can have her clothes fitted here, she can try on a hat, and if she doesn't want it she doesn't have to keep it; go anywhere on the cars after I pay my fare; I can do any sort of work I know how to do.
4. Yes, go anywhere I please, buy what I please; ain't afraid to get on cars and sit where I please.
5. Well, I make more money. I can't save anything from it. There are so many places to go here.
6. Yes. More places to go, parks and playgrounds for children, no differences made between colored and white.
7. Have money to get whatever is desired. Live in a better house and can go places denied at home.
8. Don't have to look up to the white man.
9. Don't have to go to the buzzard roost [Jim Crow seating in the balcony of southern theaters].
10. No lynching; no fear of mobs; can express myself and defend myself.

The commission offered detailed case histories on the experience of a few black families. One of them focused on "Mr. J.," a 49-year-old former resident of Henry County, Georgia, his 38-year-old wife, and their 21-year-old daughter. Mr. J. had come to Chicago in February 1917, seeking better work; he found it in the stockyards, and later in a mill where he was employed as an ironworker making $30 a week, six times what he had earned as a sharecropper in the South. They rented a six-room house on South Park Avenue. When the daughter married, her husband moved in with them. And a nephew of Mr. J. also boarded in the apartment. The account, published in *The Negro in Chicago*, continued:

> The whole family belongs to the Salem Baptist Church and attends twice a week. The wife is a member of the Pastor's Aid and the Willing Workers Club, also the Elk's Lodge. The husband is a member of the Knights of Pythias. He goes to the parks, bathing-beaches and baseball games for amusement. The family spends much of its time in church and helped to establish the "Come and See" Baptist Mission at East Thirty-first Street and Cottage Grove Avenue. They have gone to a show only once or twice since they came to the city. During the summer they spend Sunday afternoons at the East Twenty-ninth Street Beach. . . . The wife thinks that northern Negroes have better manners, but are not as friendly as the colored people in the South. She says people do not visit each other, and one is never invited to dine at a friend's house. She thinks they cannot afford it with food so high. She thinks people were better in the South than they are here and says they had to be good there for they had nothing else to do but go to church. She feels a greater freedom here because of the right to vote, the better treatment accorded by white people, the lack of "Jim Crow" laws. She likes the North because of the protection afforded by the law and the better working conditions. "You don't have an overseer always standing over you," she remarked. Life here is harder, however, because one has to work all the time. "In the South you could rest occasionally, but here, where food is so high and one must pay cash, it is hard to come out even." The climate is colder, making it necessary to buy more clothes and coal. Rent also is very

much higher here. . . . With all this, Mrs. J. gets more pleasure from her income because the necessities of life here were luxuries in Georgia, and though such things are dear here there is money to pay for them. . . . She hopes that an equal chance in industry will be given to all; that more houses will be provided for the people and rent will be charged for the worth of the house; and the cost of living generally will be reduced. She does not expect to return to Georgia and is advising friends to come to Chicago.

NOTES

pp. 63–64 "I saw a million people . . ." Quoted in James Grossman, *Land of Hope: Chicago, Black Southerners, and the Great Migration* (Chicago: University of Chicago Press, 1991), p. 115.

p. 67 "crowds surge, weaving currents . . ." *New Republic*, Nov. 20, 1915, p. 71.

p. 69 "South State Street was . . ." Quoted in Grossman, *Land of Hope*, p. 117.

p. 71 "probably the strongest effective unit . . ." Quoted in William Tuttle, *Race Riot: Chicago in the Red Summer of 1919* (New York: Atheneum, 1970), p. 184.

p. 76 "You notice there ain't no Jim Crow . . ." Quoted in Tuttle, *Race Riot*, p. 137.

p. 77 "Chicago's colored population is growing . . ." Quoted in Junius Boyd Wood, *The Negro in Chicago*. (Chicago: Chicago Daily News, 1916), pp. 23–24.

p. 77–78 "Many of the buildings . . ." Quoted in Junius Boyd Wood, *The Negro in Chicago*. (Chicago: Chaicago Daily News, 1916), pp. 23–24.

p. 79 "Every colored man who moves . . ." Quoted in Chicago Commission on Race Relations, *The Negro in Chicago: A Study of Race Relations and a Race Riot* (Chicago: University of Chicago Press, 1922), p. 121.

p. 84 "Finally, the new spirit aroused . . ." Quoted in Herbert Aptheker, ed., *A Documentary History of the Negro People in the United States, 1910–1932*, Vol. II (Secaucus, N.J.: Citadel Press, 1973), pp. 277–278.

p. 85 "We don't 'low no . . ." Quoted in Arnold Rampersad, *The Life of Langston Hughes, I Too, Sing America, 1902–1941*, Vol. I (New York: Oxford University Press, 1986), p. 27.

p. 85 "The migration of Negroes from South to North continues . . ." Reprinted in David Levering Lewis, ed., *W. E. B. DuBois: A Reader* (New York: Henry Holt and Co., 1995), pp. 529–530.

p. 86 "1. Yes. Living in better houses, . . ." Quoted in Drake and Cayton, *Black Metropolis*, pp. 99–100.

p. 87 "The whole family belongs . . ." Chicago Commission on Race Relations, *The Negro in Chicago*, pp. 171–172.

6

"The Fat Years Were at Hand": The Growth of the Black Metropolis

The First World War ended with the armistice on November 11, 1918. American soldiers in France left the muddy trenches of the western front behind them, reboarded the troop ships that had carried them across the Atlantic, and returned to a jubilant welcome in the United States. Among the conquering heroes were Harlem's own 369th U.S. Infantry, a unit that spent more time in the front lines than any other in the American Expeditionary Force. The 369th was the first American infantry regiment to march in triumph through the streets of New York City at war's end. As the doughboys, black and white alike, marched down the great avenues of New York and other American cities in victory parades, they were showered by confetti and cheered by crowds of deliriously happy spectators. Veterans and civilians alike felt that the postwar world was going to be a time filled with opportunities, excitement, and change. As one popular song of the era put it, "How you going to keep 'em down on the farm/once they've seen gay Par-ee?"

But not all veterans were equally welcomed or honored as they returned to their hometowns. The war to preserve political democracy in Europe had not brought racial democracy to the American southland. Throughout the region, southern whites were determined to reassert authority over an increasingly restive black population. In 1919 there were 76 lynchings of black men in the South. A dozen of the victims were war veterans, still wearing military uniforms. Among those who received a sharp reminder of local racial customs when they returned home was William Lee Conley Broonzy (who would become better known as the blues musician "Big Bill" Broonzy). He had taken the train to his hometown in Arkansas after military service in France. But this time there were no grateful civilians waiting to welcome him home:

> I got off the train at this place—had a nice uniform [and] everything and I met a white fellow that was knowing me before I went in the army and so he told me, "Listen, boy," he says, "now you been in the army?"
> I told him, "Yeah."
> He says, "How did you like it?"
> I said, "It's okay."
> He says, "Well, you ain't in the army now." Says, "And those clothes you got there," says, "you can take [them] off and get you some overhalls," says, "because there's no nigger gonna walk around here with no Uncle Sam's uniform on, see, up and down *these* streets."

In some ways the Red Summer of 1919 and the years that followed resembled the end of the Reconstruction era. Just as Frederick Douglass' hope that service in the Civil War would secure equal rights for the freedmen ended in bitter disappointment in the 1870s, so a half century later did W. E. B. DuBois' hope that by standing "shoulder to shoulder" with their fellow white citizens, African Americans would achieve the same end.

But if history seemed to be repeating itself, this time there was one important difference. Unlike the 1870s, African Americans were no longer exclusively a rural southern people. Many of them now lived in the urban North, where they were fashioning new forms of cultural and political expression for themselves. Within a year of returning to Arkansas, Big Bill Broonzy had caught a freight train to Chicago, where he would live for most of the rest of his life. Three quarters of a million southern blacks made similar choices in the 1920s. Although sparked by wartime labor scarcity, the Great Migration scarcely missed a beat with the coming of peace. Although only 10 percent of the nation's population, black Americans accounted for 20 percent of all interstate migration in the decade following the war. They traveled not only by train, but as highways improved, by bus and automobile. Jobs in the North in the 1920s were not as plentiful as in

> White men who have struggled for and built up their countries and their own civilizations are not disposed to hand them over to the Negro or any other race without let or hindrance. It would be unreasonable to expect this. Hence any vain assumption on the part of the Negro to imagine that he will one day become President of the Nation, Governor of the State, or Mayor of the City in the countries of white men, is like waiting on the devil and his angels to take up their residence in the Realm on High and direct there the affairs of Paradise."
>
> ◆
>
> —Marcus Garvey, 1923, on the possibility of black advancement through the ballot box

1917–18 (and, indeed, in 1921–22 the nation's basic industries were gripped by postwar recession, and black workers —last hired and first fired—suffered an unemployment rate twice that of their white counterparts). But if the pull of economic opportunity lessened, the push of southern racism remained as powerful as ever. And, as the economy picked up in the years that followed, so did the demand for black labor—especially since Congress sharply limited further immigration from abroad with the passage of the National Origins Act in 1924. In Chicago's steel mills and packinghouses in the 1920s, for example, blacks accounted for a larger proportion of the manufacturing force than they did for the city's population.

By this time there was no need to send industrial recruiters south to spread the word of opportunities in northern cities. The most effective recruiters were southern blacks who had already made the journey northward. Visits "down home" for family celebrations, or during temporary or seasonal layoffs from work, became a regular fixture of life in the new black communities in the North. And the example set by these visitors from the North, who came bearing gifts, dressing well, sometimes driving their own automobiles, and carrying themselves with pride and dignity was a powerful inducement to those who had remained behind. By decade's end more than four out of every ten African Americans lived in the nation's cities, North and South. The black populations of New York and Chicago each doubled during the 1920s. Only the coming of the Great Depression in 1929 would slow the exodus, and then only temporarily. As the African-American sociologists St. Clair Drake and Horace R. Cayton wrote in their classic 1945 study *Black Metropolis*: "The Black Belt became the Black Metropolis in the twenty years between the close of the First World War and the beginning of the Second."

What was life like in the black metropolises of the North in the "Roaring Twenties"? Many of the hardships that blacks had met on first arriving in the big cities of the North remained in effect. Housing was still in short supply and often of substandard quality. White residents continued to meet with hostility and violence attempts by black tenants and homeowners to move into their neighborhoods. African-American workers were excluded altogether from some skilled crafts and some trade unions, and relegated to the lowest rungs of most industries. Life in the black metropolis was surely no crystal stair.

Despite all that, the 1920s proved a vital and optimistic era for urban African Americans. Looking back from the perspective of the end of the Second World War, Drake and Cayton pronounced the years from 1924 to 1929 to be undoubtedly "the most prosperous ones the Negro community in Chicago had ever experienced":

> A professional and business class arose upon the broad base of over seventy-five thousand colored wage-earners, and was able for a brief period to enjoy the fruits of its training and investment. Throughout the Twenties additional migrants from the rural South swelled the size of the Black Belt market. The Fat Years were at hand.

Fat years also came to what poet, novelist and NAACP secretary James Weldon Johnson called "the greatest Negro city in the world," New York City. At the turn of the century, New York had lacked a concentrated African-American residential center like Chicago's black belt. Instead, black residents could be found spread throughout a 40-block region of what would later be considered midtown Manhattan. They usually occupied a segregated block or two of buildings scattered among white working-class neighborhoods. There was also a significant black community in Brooklyn, which for many years was considered the cultural center of New York black life.

At the turn of the century, only a few blacks lived in Harlem, a prosperous suburb of the city filled with luxurious townhouses and apartment buildings. Most could not afford to do so. But when a speculative boom in Harlem real estate suddenly collapsed in 1904–05, landlords began to encourage black tenants to move northward from the crowded districts of mid-Manhattan. Many of the newcomers paid extortionate rents for crowded quarters. Nonetheless, unlike the crumbling wooden tenements of Chicago's South Side and other urban black communities that grew up on the former sites of immigrant working-class neighborhoods, Harlem's housing stock was magnificent. In James Weldon Johnson's words, black Harlemites enjoyed "better, cleaner, more modern, more airy, more sunny houses than they ever lived in before."

As blacks began moving to Harlem, churches, merchants, and professionals followed. The NAACP, the national Urban League, and such influential black newspapers as the *Amsterdam News* set up headquarters in Harlem. Black-owned theaters and restaurants opened along Lenox Avenue, providing a lively night life. The influx of African Americans in the prewar years prompted white flight until, by the time of the armistice, the district "tipped" to a majority black population. Among Harlem's distinctive features was its international flavor, with perhaps as many as a quarter of its black population in the 1920s consisting of migrants from the West Indies. By 1920 two-thirds of Manhattan's black population, native-born and West Indian, lived in Harlem.

And it was within this community that the "Harlem Renaissance" took off. New York City, long the nation's cultural capital, now became black America's as well. African-American poets, novelists, critics, playwrights, and musicians flocked to the city. There they benefited from the patronage of both black and white audiences. And for the most part they could appeal to this racially diverse audience without having to tailor their art to the expectations of whites. Black artists and cultural critics like Alain Locke, James Weldon Johnson, Jean Toomer, Countee Cullen, and Zora Neale Hurston considered themselves the vanguard of the "New Negro," proud of their African heritage and determined to be treated as political and cultural equals in postwar America. As the poet Langston Hughes, among the most prominent figures in the Harlem Renaissance, declared in an article in 1926:

> One of the most promising of young Negro poets said to me once, "I want to be a poet—not a Negro poet," meaning, I believe, "I want to write like a white poet"; meaning subconsciously, "I would like to be a white poet"; meaning behind that, "I would like to be white." And I was sorry the young man said that, for no great poet has ever been afraid of himself. And I doubted then that, with his desire to run away spiritually from his race, this boy would ever be a great poet. But this is the mountain standing in the way of any true Negro art in America—this urge within the race toward whiteness, the desire to pour racial individuality into the mold of American standardization, and to be as little Negro and as much American as possible.

The fact that the 1920s are sometimes referred to as the "Jazz Age," and that the best-known dance craze of the decade was "the Charleston," which began as a black dance, testifies to the new importance of African Americans in the nation's consciousness and culture. Many whites were curious about black culture. For some it was just an exotic escape from the Puritan aspects of the era of Prohibition (the Cotton Club, a famous Harlem night spot, catered exclusively to white audiences). But on a deeper level, American music, dance, and language was beginning to be profoundly influenced by African-American culture.

Jazz, a fusion of southern blues and New Orleans ragtime with brass-band music and syncopated dance music, took the nation by storm in the 1920s. The Great Migration ushered in an era of great black musicians. Many of the principal performers of the era, like Louis Armstrong, had been born in the South; and whether southern-born or not, it was the growth of the black metropolises in the North that gave them a mass audience and national visibility. "Race records" began to appear in 1920, when Mamie Smith and the Jazz Hounds recorded "You Can't Keep a Good Man Down" and "This Thing Called Love" in a New York City Studio. Harry Pace, who moved from Memphis to New York City during the Great Migration, set up the first black-owned recording company in 1921, pressing records on the Black Swan label. Meanwhile radio stations in Chicago and New York began broadcasting live performances by groups like Fletcher Henderson's Rainbow Orchestra. The demand for such music led to the appearance of white imitators, but also provided steady employment for a generation of blues and jazz musicians from the black community.

New York and Chicago competed as centers of African-American music. New York enjoyed the lead in the "big bands" of the era, as home to Fletcher Henderson, Cab Calloway, Duke Ellington, and many others. Chicago could claim the distinction of being home to Charles "Doc" Cooke and Earl "Fatha" Hines. It was a healthy rivalry. But when it came to the blues, no one could challenge Chicago's preeminence.

The blues originated on plantations and "juke joints" along the Mississippi Delta in the 1890s, derived from and sharing features with work songs and other traditional black music. It was based on a distinctive twelve-bar, three-chord blues scale. Like most African-American music, it was singer-oriented, with a solo vocalist accompanied by guitar (later electric guitar), or piano, or small rhythm and blues (R & B) combos. The blues was a music of suffering and redemption, just like gospel, but its themes were usually secular rather than sacred: unfaithful women, hard drinking, bad jobs or no jobs, debt, natural disasters, jail, violence. W. C. Handy

"Big Bill" Broonzy

"Big Bill" Broonzy was born in Scott, Mississippi, in 1893. He was one of 17 children, raised in a sharecropper's family in rural Mississippi and Arkansas. His father, a deacon in the Baptist church, disapproved of his son's interest in what he regarded as the "devil's music," so Big Bill did not receive any encouragement at home to pursue his interest in the blues. He constructed his first musical instrument, a fiddle, out of an old cigar box. After service in the war, Broonzy moved in 1920 to Chicago, where he supported himself with a variety of odd jobs while establishing his reputation as a master of blues guitar. After years of honing his musical style in house rent parties (where tenants in an apartment would charge admission to a party, or sell drinks by the glass, to raise their month's rent) and other obscure venues, he cut a record that was released as "House Rent Stomp" in 1929. He went on to record over 250 blues songs, including classics such as "The Sun Gonna Shine in My Back Door Someday," "Keep Your Hands Off Her," and "Black, Brown, and White Blues." Broonzy's blues ranged in subject from unhappy love to politics. As he sang in his blues "Just a Dream," recorded in 1932: "I dreamed I was in the White House/Settin on the president's chair./I dreamed he shake my hand,/Said 'Old Bill, I'm glad you're here.'/But it was a dream, man,/Just a dream I had on my mind./When I woke up next morning,/Jim Crow did I find." Broonzy's quintet, the Memphis Five, helped shape the distinctive sound of Chicago Blues, with its big-city themes, and nostalgia for the rural South. Broonzy died in Chicago in 1958. ◆

(whose "Memphis Blues" was the first published blues song in 1912) and Jelly Roll Morton were among the pioneer blues performers.

Women as well as men sang the blues. Bessie Smith, Ma Rainey, Ethel Waters among the most famous. Many blues songs touched on an aspect of black migration that particularly affected women, being left behind. In 1924 Clara Smith (dubbed "the Queen of the Moaners") recorded her classic "Freight Train Blues":

> I hate to hear that engine blow, boo hoo.
> I hate to hear that engine blow, boo hoo.
> Everytime I hear it blowin, I feel like ridin too. . . .
> When a woman gets the blues she goes to her room and
> hides.
> When a woman gets the blues she goes to her room and
> hides.
> When a man gets the blues he catch the freight train and
> rides.

The Blues had several regional styles, but the most famous were the Mississippi Delta blues, which fed directly into urban blues in Chicago. Among the originators of Chicago blues was "Big Bill" Broonzy, another veteran of the Great Migration.

Athletics were another area for achievement and self-assertion for urban blacks in the 1920s. Like most other institutions in American society, professional sports had fallen victim to the spread of Jim Crow in the late 19th century. While in the years just after the Civil War blacks and whites had competed as equals on the nation's fledgling baseball teams, by century's end segregation had become the rule. The same was true for professional football, basketball, and horse racing. At the amateur level, a few black college athletes, like Rutgers' football star Paul Robeson, played on integrated teams, but southern college teams usually refused to play integrated northern teams. One of the few sports in which blacks and whites still competed in the early decades of the 20th century was professional boxing. Jack Johnson became the first black heavyweight boxing champion in 1908, and defended his title numerous times against "great white hopes" until losing it in 1915. (He was the last black

Black packinghouse workers at Swift's Premium in Chicago formed this baseball team, which played in the city's industrial baseball league during and after the First World War. (Chicago Commission on Race Relations, *The Negro in Chicago*, 1920, p. 292)

to hold the title until Joe Louis—born in Alabama and raised in Detroit—won it back in the 1930s.)

But the Great Migration created new opportunities for black athletes, especially in the "Negro leagues" of professional baseball. Northern urban blacks were eager to root for their own athletes. The Negro National League was founded in Kansas City in 1920, with six all-black baseball teams affiliating, including the Kansas City Monarchs and the Chicago American Giants. A second league, the Eastern Colored League, was established in 1923, and teams from the two leagues would compete in the later 1920s at the end of each season in a "Black World Series." The teams would often go on "barnstorming" tours of cities that lacked their own professional teams, playing challenge matches, including some against white teams. Players like pitcher Satchel Paige of the powerful Pittsburgh Crawfords became celebrities in the black community. The Negro leagues proved to be one of the great black economic success stories of the era (many though not all the teams were black-owned). The Negro leagues also contributed to the vitality of the black press—since the major white-owned newspapers generally ignored the black leagues, fans from around the country subscribed to black newspapers like the *Chicago Defender* or the *Pittsburgh Courier* to keep up with the exploits of their favorite teams and players.

In politics, as in literature, music, and sports, northern blacks found new means of self-expression in the 1920s. Under the leadership of Marcus Garvey, a massive, if short-lived black nationalist movement took shape in the 1920s. Garvey, who was born in Jamaica in 1887, founded the Universal Negro Improvement Association (UNIA) in 1914, an organization with a Booker T. Washington–like emphasis on black self-help. But when Garvey moved to Harlem during the First World War, he began to preach a new message—Pan-Africanism. Garvey argued that the well-being of blacks in the United States, Jamaica, and throughout the world depended on the creation of strong, independent black nations in Africa. His was a gospel of racial pride and racial solidarity, to be achieved through a practical program of creating black-owned businesses. Contrary to myth, he never argued that all blacks had to do was go "back to Africa." Rather, he foresaw a gradual process of building black nationhood in Africa, aided by the material resources provided by blacks living in the New World.

Garvey's message struck a responsive chord among the migrants who were crowding in to the new black communities in the North. As one wrote home:

> Yesterday afternoon I went to a meeting of the Universal Negro Improvement Association which is headed by Garvey. . . . They say without a country of their own, strong, able, and willing to protect Negroes everywhere, they will always suffer. I think they are about right about that. . . . I sometimes wonder if this organization is not

the seed of a Nationalist movement of Negro Peoples? You should see their flag of pure silk in red, black, and green, the color runs across the flag, each a third of it. The black represents the Negro or black race, the red sacrifice, and the green eternal hope. Their songs are quite stirring and some parts are really wonderful.

At its peak, the UNIA had over 100,000 dues-paying members, and estimates of its support range into the millions. Twenty-five thousand people attended its 1920 national convention. Garvey's organization was based in New York City, but maintained outposts in larger black communities across the United States, as well as in the West Indies and Africa.

In pursuit of the goal of economic independence, the UNIA created an array of commercial enterprises, including hotels, printing plants, groceries, restaurants, and laundries. Garvey's best-known business was a shipping company, the Black Star Line. Garvey hoped not only to turn a profit with the Black Star Line, but also to use its ships to foster black American commerce with and migration to Africa. But the Black Star Line proved a financial disaster. Economic separatism and "buy black" campaigns foundered on the African-American community's lack of capital and other resources to sustain anything like a self-sufficient economy. Banks were often reluctant to

"So you're going north, hunh?"

"Yes, sir. My family's taking me with 'em."

"The North's no good for your people, boy."

"I'll try to get along, sir." . . .

"How're you going to act up there?"

"Just like I act down here, sir."

"Would you speak to a white girl up there?"

"Oh, no, sir. I'll act there just like I act here."

"Aw, no, you won't. You'll change. Niggers change when they go north."

◆

—Richard Wright, *Black Boy*, reaction of his white employer in Memphis when he announced he was moving to Chicago lend money to black businesses. And the small scale of most black-owned retail stores prevented them from buying in bulk, putting them at a competitive disadvantage.

Garvey's economic woes were compounded by political missteps. In a move that was highly and understandably controversial in the black community, Garvey met in 1922 with the imperial wizard of the Ku Klux Klan (KKK), seeking financial aid from the Klan for the Black Star Line. He argued that the two groups, each committed to racial separatism, had much in common. If the KKK wanted to make America "a white man's country," Garvey's movement was equally committed to the vision of a black-ruled Africa, so there was no reason the two could not work together.

Garvey's critics in the black community included W. E. B. DuBois and others who wanted blacks to fight for their rights as American citizens, not to entertain fantasies about moving back to Africa. Garvey's black opponents were also critical of his personal excesses, such as his habits of dressing up in ornate pseudo-military uniforms and referring to himself as "lord high potentate" of the movement. The Harlem *Messenger*, a radical black newspaper, denounced him as the "Supreme Negro Jamaican Jackass." Garvey might have weathered his economic and political troubles had he not at the same time become embroiled in legal difficulties. He was convicted on mail-fraud charges connected with the sale of Black Star Line stock, imprisoned in 1925, and deported from the United States in 1927. Although the Garveyite movement soon faded into organizational oblivion, it had a lasting political influence. Some former Garveyites found their way into the newly organized Black Muslims in the 1930s, and in the 1960s Malcolm X was among those who cited Garvey's memory as inspiration for his own brand of black nationalism.

The "fat years" of the new black metropolises came to an abrupt end with the stock market crash of 1929 and the nation's subsequent economic descent into the Great

Depression. In the 1920s the demand for consumer goods, like phonographs and Model T Fords, had kept the economy humming. But wages had not kept pace with industrial productivity. Most consumer purchases, even of smaller items like radios, had been made on credit: installment buying was one of the marketing innovations of the decade. By the end of the 1920s Americans were deeply in debt, and consumer demand began to decline dramatically. That led to layoffs in manufacturing, which depressed demand even further, until the economy entered a tailspin from which some believed it would never recover. Millions of Americans lost their jobs, their savings, and their homes. The national unemployment rate climbed to over a quarter of the work-force by the spring of 1933, when Franklin Delano Roosevelt was inaugurated president of the United States; among African-American workers it was twice as high.

In the midst of the nation's greatest economic crisis, some turned to radical solutions. Drake and Cayton reported in *Black Metropolis*:

> Throughout the Twenties, Black Metropolis had been hearing new voices talking to the Negro people, voices that spoke strange words: "proletarian," "bourgeoisie," "class struggle," "revolution." . . . Most of the Negroes in Black Metropolis were too busy enjoying the lush Twenties to pay much attention to these "Reds" or "Communists." But in the early Thirties they began to listen. . . . The Communists began a vigorous program of organization in the Black Belt, forming neighborhood Unemployment Councils to demand adequate relief. It was these Councils that led the fight against evictions, and hundreds of non-Communists followed their lead. When eviction notices arrived, it was not unusual for a mother to shout to the children, "Run quick and find the Reds!"

Some prominent black intellectuals like Langston Hughes were sympathetic to the communist movement; Hughes would contribute a poem entitled "Good Morning Revolution" to a communist magazine in 1934, and sent back enthusiastic reports from a tour he took of the Soviet Union. Many black industrial workers joined unions, like the Packinghouse Workers, in which communists were active as leaders and organizers. But relatively few blacks actually joined the party. The most significant change in black political loyalties in the 1930s came about thanks to President Roosevelt and his New Deal policies.

On the eve of the Great Depression, most black voters were still loyal Republicans. The Democrats were the party of white supremacy and the solid South; the Republicans were the party of Lincoln and emancipation. When Chicago voters sent a black man, Oscar DePriest, to Congress in 1928 —the first black to be elected to that body in the 20th century —he was a Republican. Robert Abbott, publisher of the *Chicago Defender*, had used his newspaper to endorse every Republican presidential candidate from William Howard Taft in 1908 to Herbert Hoover in 1928. Hoover gained 75 percent of the votes of black Chicagoans in 1928, despite the fact that he had also won (and not repudiated) the endorsement of the Ku Klux Klan. (The Klan opposed the Democratic nominee, New York governor Al Smith, because Smith was a Roman Catholic and an outspoken critic of the Klan.) In 1932 many blacks regarded the Democratic nominee Franklin Roosevelt with suspicion. His political record did not suggest any sympathy for the plight of black Americans; indeed, when he served as assistant secretary of the navy during the presidential administration of Woodrow Wilson, Roosevelt had been responsible for the construction of segregated toilets in the State, War, and Navy Department buildings in Washington, D.C. The *Defender* endorsed Hoover in 1932, despite his unpopularity because of the

Great Depression, and labeled Roosevelt "the weakest possible candidate."

But others felt differently. Robert Vann, publisher of the *Pittsburgh Courier* and a Roosevelt adviser in the 1932 election campaign, advised his readers to "go home and turn Lincoln's picture to the wall. The debt has been paid in full." And in the next four years, Roosevelt's policies led to a mass defection of black voters from the Republican Party. New Deal programs like the Public Works Administration (PWA), the Works Progress Administration (WPA), and the Civilian Conservation Corps (CCC), provided jobs and sustenance for millions of unemployed Americans. In some regions benefits were unevenly distributed, with blacks getting less than whites. But even so, no federally sponsored programs since the days of the Freedmen's Bureau had done so much for the black community. The political impact was already evident in 1934 when Oscar DePriest's political career came to an abrupt end when he was replaced by a black Democratic congressman, Arthur Mitchell—the first black Democrat ever to sit in Congress. In 1936 Roosevelt received over three quarters of the black vote, and even the *Chicago Defender* finally got around to endorsing Roosevelt when he ran in 1940 for an unprecedented third term in office.

Notwithstanding Roosevelt's popularity in the black community, the overall impact of the New Deal on African Americans was decidedly mixed. As a measure to bolster sagging prices for agricultural products, the Agricultural Adjustment Administration (AAA) provided cash subsidies to landowners who took land out of production. Many southern and southwestern landowners responded by turning sharecroppers and tenants off their land. They also used their checks from the government to buy tractors and other farm machinery, eliminating the need for agricultural workers. As a result, hundreds of thousands of rural Americans were left without any hope of employment unless they moved elsewhere. The best-known examples were the "Okies"—the white tenant farmers and sharecroppers who headed off for California in their beat-up jalopies, and whose memory was preserved in John Steinbeck's famous novel of the 1930s, *The Grapes of Wrath*. But hundreds of thousands of blacks as well as whites were similarly affected; 400,000 more southern blacks joined the "Great Migration" northwards during the 1930s. The black metropolises of the North continued to grow, through fat and lean years alike. And the greatest wave of black migration was still to come.

NOTES

p. 91   "I got off the train . . ." Quoted in Alan Lomax, *The Land Where the Blues Began* (New York: Pantheon Books, 1993), p. 435.

p. 93   "The Black Belt became . . ." St. Clair Drake and Horace R. Cayton, *Black Metropolis: A Study of Negro Life in a Northern City*, Vol. I, rev. ed., (New York: Harcourt, Brace and World, 1962), p. 77.

p. 94   "A professional and business class arose . . ." Drake and Cayton, *Black Metropolis*, p. 78.

p. 96   "One of the most promising . . ." Quoted in Herbert Aptheker, ed., *A Documentary History of the Negro People in the United States, 1910–1932*, Vol. II (Secaucus, N.J.: Citadel Press, 1973), p. 526.

p. 98   "I dreamed I was in the White House . . ." Quoted in Lomax, *Land Where the Blues Began*, p. 457.

p. 99   "I hate to hear that engine blow . . ." Quoted in Hazel V. Carby, "'It Jus Be's Dat Way Sometime': The Sexual Politics of Women's Blues," in Ellen Carol DuBois and Vicki L. Ruiz, *Unequal Sisters: A Multicultural Reader in U.S. Women's History* (New York: Routledge, 1990), p. 243.

p. 101   "Yesterday afternoon I went . . ." Quoted in Spencer R. Crew, *Field to Factory: Afro-American Migration 1915–1940* (Washington, D.C.: Smithsonian Institution, 1987), p. 63.

p. 104   "Throughout the Twenties . . ." Drake and Cayton, *Black Metropolis*, pp. 86–87.

p. 106   "go home and turn . . ." Quoted in Leslie H. Fishel, Jr., "The Negro in the New Deal Era," in Bernard Sternsher, ed., *The Negro in Depression and War* (Chicago: Quadrangle Books, 1969), p. 8.

7

The End of the
Great Migration

The term *Great Migration,* used by historians to describe the northward movement of African Americans between World War I and the Great Depression, can be somewhat misleading. The migration of a million and a half African Americans in those years was indeed "great" in comparison with earlier periods. But in sheer numbers, the northward movement of African Americans in the 30 years from 1940 to 1970 dwarfed that of the preceding era. In 1940, over three quarters of black Americans still lived in the South. Just under half lived in the rural South. Over the next 30 years, 5 million blacks moved to the North and the West. One and a half million made the journey in the 1950s alone. By 1970, as a result, only half of all

African Americans continued to reside in the South, and only a quarter of them lived in rural communities.

Blacks left the South in these decades for both old and new reasons. During World War II, opportunities in the burgeoning defense industries beckoned to poorly paid southern sharecroppers and domestic workers. President Franklin Roosevelt, pressured by black trade union leader A. Philip Randolph, issued Executive Order 8808 in the summer of 1941, forbidding employment discrimination in war industries. The federal government established a Fair Employment Practices Commission (FEPC) to enforce compliance with the order. Not since the days of the Freedmen's Bureau had Washington, D.C., played as direct a role in preserving and extending the rights of African Americans. Federal agencies such as the War Manpower Commission, the War Production Board, and the United States Employment Service recruited rural blacks to work in urban defense industries.

Hundreds of thousands of southern blacks swelled the wartime populations of the existing black metropolises in Chicago, Detroit, New York City, and elsewhere. Others broke new ground. The West Coast became an important center of shipbuilding and aircraft construction during World War II. In the first wave of the Great Migration, relatively few African Americans had moved to cities west of the Mississippi River. Not so this time, as hundreds of thousands of black pioneers made their way to Los Angeles, San Francisco, Oakland, Portland, Seattle, and other western destinations. California alone attracted 340,000 black migrants between 1940 and 1945.

Once again in the Second World War, as in the first, blacks were called upon to defend their country. Nearly a million had gone into uniform by 1945. Once again, despite the fact that they served in segregated units, many veterans returned home with a broader sense of the world and the kind of personal aspirations that they could not hope to realize in the rural South. And, as in the earlier period, letters from and visits home by northern kin encouraged many black southerners to move North.

But the character of this second great migration changed in some important ways, particularly in the years that followed the war. Along with the pull of economic opportunity, the later migration was also the product of the push of changing agricultural practices and land use in South. Instead of black migrants having to ignore the threats or inducements from southern whites to stay, this time blacks were being evicted by white landowners who no longer had any use for them as labor supply. Southern white landowners, who had bitterly resisted the first Great Migration, became in effect among the instigators of the second.

Cotton growing had always been a labor-intensive enterprise, particularly in its harvesting. Workers had to be available to go out in the fields and remove the soft, white, downy fibers that surrounded the seeds in the cotton boll. The work that had been done by the unfree labor of black slaves in the years leading up to emancipation had been performed by the quasi-free labor of black sharecroppers ever since. While other staple crops, like wheat and corn, lent themselves to mechanical harvesting, cotton did not. Despite decades of efforts to develop a mechanical cotton picker, it was only in 1944 that the first practical working model was tried out in a Mississippi cotton field. That model proved capable of picking as much cotton in a day as 50 handpickers. And, as a result, the economy of the South, and the demography of the country, was about to change dramatically.

Mechanical cotton pickers were an expensive investment, and their introduction took time; as late as 1958 less than a third of the cotton crop in the Mississippi Delta region was harvested by mechanical pickers. But the competitive advantage of mechanical picking could not be ignored forever. In the late 1950s and early 1960s there was a rush to obtain the machines; by 1964 more than four-fifths of the cotton in the Mississippi Delta was harvested by the new machines. Other agricultural innovations, like the introduction of chemical weed killers, eliminated the need for hand hoeing of cotton. And many southern planters switched from cotton production to the profitable soybean crop in these years; compared to cotton, soybeans grew practically untended by human hands. The result of these various innovations was the virtual elimination of sharecropping. (Many poor southern whites were also affected by these changes, as well as by the increased mechanization of the Appalachian coal-mining industry. The southern diaspora to the cities of the North in the second half of the 20th century was a white as well as a black phenomenon.)

The black metropolises of the prewar years were small towns compared to what would come in the postwar era. In 1940 the black population of Chicago stood at 277,000, or 6.9 percent of the city's population of 3.4 million. By 1960 it had grown to 812,637, or 22.9 percent of the city's population of 3.55 million. And by 1970, it stood at over 1.1 million, over a third of the city's population of 3.3 million. More African Americans lived in the city of Chicago than in the entire state of Mississippi.

The growth of the black population in the North had important political consequences for blacks and whites alike. The 1950s saw the beginnings of a decade-long struggle that overturned the long-entrenched system of Jim Crow segregation in the South. In 1954, in *Brown* v. *Board of Education of Topeka, Kansas*, the U.S. Supreme Court ruled that states that maintained "separate but equal" facilities in public education violated the constitutional guarantees of equal protection before the law. But the real signal that a new

Harold Washington _____

For Harold Washington, a first-generation Chicagoan, Chicago truly turned out to be the Promised Land. Washington was born in Chicago in 1922. His grandfather had been a minister in Kentucky; his father came to Chicago during the Great Migration and worked in a packinghouse before earning a law degree. Harold Washington attended DuSable High School. After his service in the Second World War he entered Roosevelt University, where he was the first black student to be elected senior class president. He went on to receive a law degree from Northwestern University, where he was the only black student in his law class. In the early 1950s he began his rise in political influence through Chicago politics. Washington was, for many years, a loyal supporter of Mayor Richard J. Daley's Democratic machine; Daley had won election as the city's mayor in 1955 with strong backing in the black community, and there were political rewards for those who helped Daley maintain his secure control of black voters. Washington was elected to the Illinois House of Representatives in 1964, and he held that office until his successful run for Illinois State Senate in 1976.

In the late 1960s, Washington began to challenge the Daley machine on selected issues. He supported, for example, the creation of a civilian police review board, a proposal with strong support in the black community. He also helped organize the Illinois Legislative Black Caucus. In 1977, in a dramatic break with the Democratic machine, Washington ran in the Democratic primary for mayor of Chicago, in a special election called after Mayor Daley's death. Though defeated, he went on to win

political era was dawning came in 1955–56, when the black citizens of Montgomery, Alabama, under the leadership of Dr. Martin Luther King, Jr., launched a successful year-long boycott of the city's segregated public transportation system. The success of the bus boycott was due, first and foremost, to the sacrifice and courage of the black citizens of Montgomery. But the boycott was also sustained by the reelection to the state Senate, and in 1980 was elected to the United States Congress, where he was a highly visible spokesperson for black and liberal causes.

In the fall of 1982 he entered the Democratic mayoral primary, running against the incumbent mayor Jane Byrne and Richard M. Daley, son of the late mayor. Thanks to a voter registration drive and an upswelling of support in the black community, he won a plurality of the primary vote. In the general election of 1983, the Republican candidate made an unexpectedly strong showing due to white voter defections from the Democratic column, but Washington nonetheless proved the victor with 51.5 percent of the vote in a record-breaking voter turnout. Washington's victory, not only electrified the black community in Chicago, but was hailed as a decisive political triumph for all of black America. The editors of Ebony magazine compared the significance of Washington's victory to Martin Luther King Jr.'s "I Have a Dream" speech in Washington 20 years earlier.

Washington's first term in office proved a stormy one. He was at odds with many of the Democratic machine loyalists on the city council. Nonetheless, he proved a popular and effective mayor. Among other achievements, he pushed through campaign finance reform measures and appointed Chicago's first black police chief. In the spring of 1987 he was reelected as mayor with 54 percent of the vote. But on November 25 of that year, the day before Thanksgiving, Mayor Washington suffered a massive heart attack and died at his desk. At his funeral, the Chicago Housing Authority's youth choir brought tears to the eyes of many of the mourners with their touching rendition of the spiritual "Keep on Moving." ◆

financial and political support of blacks, and of sympathetic whites, in the North. In the years that followed, Dr. King would spend almost as much time in the North, fund-raising and building a broad coalition in support of the movement, as he would in such centers of the civil rights struggle as Birmingham and Selma. Thousands of black and white volunteers from the North came down to lend a hand most notably during the "Freedom Rides" of 1961 and the "Freedom Summer" of 1964. Influential white politicians in the North who previously had shown little interest in the cause of civil rights now found it expedient to respond to the concerns of their black constituents. As a result, civil rights became the most important domestic issue for the United States in the 1960s. By the end of the decade, public schools, public transportation, and public accommodations were opened up on an equal basis to black and white alike. And southern blacks regained the right to vote, which had been taken from them in the aftermath of Reconstruction. Blacks won political offices throughout the South, from county sheriffs to U.S. congressional representatives. In the North, in the same period, blacks also made striking gains in political power, electing mayors in cities such as Cleveland, Newark, Detroit, and, some years later, in Chicago.

The Great Migration ushered in an era of expanding rights, opportunities, and political power for African Americans. The legacy of the Great Migration is not, however, simply one of triumph. In the last third of the 20th century, the black metropolises of the North were wracked by a series of economic and social crises.

The dramatic increase in the urban black population in the 1950s and 1960s sparked an unprecedented "white flight"—not just to other urban neighborhoods, as in the earlier era of the Great Migration, but out of the cities altogether. In the 1950s alone, the nation's 12 largest cities lost 2 million white residents, while gaining 1,800,000 nonwhite residents. The long hot summers of the 1960s— which saw deadly riots break out in the Watts neighborhood of Los Angeles in 1965, in Chicago in 1966, in Detroit and Newark in 1967, and in Washington, D.C. and a hundred other locations in the aftermath of Martin Luther King's assassination in 1968—accelerated this trend. In the minds of many Americans, the cities were no longer a promised land of opportunity and innovation, but had become instead a wasteland of failed dreams, failed policies, and failed communities. As a result, the politics of the 1980s and 1990s increasingly took the form of white Republican suburbs locked in conflict with black Democratic cities.

The federal government inadvertently helped foster these social divisions. The Federal Housing Administration (FHA), established in 1934 by President Roosevelt, provided federal insurance for residential housing mortgages. This policy encouraged private banks to lend money for housing and contributed to a postwar building boom, as did the low-interest loans made available to World War II veterans under the GI Bill. FHA and Veterans Administration (VA) mortgages provided a step up into the "American dream" for millions of families as the percentage of Americans owning their own homes jumped dramatically in these years. But FHA and VA policies encouraged the construction of new, single-family housing units in the suburbs rather than the construction or rehabilitation of multiunit apartment buildings in cities. And, until the late 1940s, the FHA maintained an official policy of encouraging racially segregated neighborhoods, warning bank officers that integration threatened the "stability" of property values. Less than 2 percent of all housing financed with federal mortgage insurance between 1946 and 1959 was sold to African Americans.

Thus, while millions of acres of farmland surrounding urban areas were bulldozed and paved over and transformed into suburban communities, the housing stock of the nation's older cities was left to crumble into disrepair. The division between shiny new thriving suburbs and dingy neglected cities deepened after 1956, when President Dwight Eisenhower signed the Federal Highway Act into law. The measure provided federal subsidies that made possible a massive interstate highway system. This too was good for the national economy—but not so good for the urban economy. The new highway system made it ever easier for people to live in one area and work in another. The commute into the central city became part of the daily routine for millions of (mostly white) suburban Americans, while urban public transportation systems, which increasingly served a clientele of poor and minority residents, were allowed to deteriorate. The same fate befell other urban services and amenities, including, most disastrously, the public school system.

In these years the economy changed in another way detrimental to the future of the black metropolises. Starting in the late 1950s, jobs in industrial manufacturing began to disappear at an alarming rate. The corporations that owned the steel mills, garment factories, shipyards, auto factories, machine shops, electrical assembly plants, and other mainstays of the 20th century urban economy increasingly contracted work out to other regions, or countries, where labor costs were lower. By the 1970s the nation's "industrial belt," stretching from New England through New York, Pennsylvania, Ohio, Michigan, and Illinois, began to be referred to as the "rust belt." From the late 1960s to the late 1980s Chicago lost 60 percent of its manufacturing jobs; New York City 58 percent; and Detroit 51 percent. Some of the more economically favored cities added jobs in service industries (e.g., finance, communications, insurance, retail sales), but these tended to provide either temporary and low-paying employment, or else be jobs that required high levels of education or training. Secure, well-paying, unionized jobs for workers without such training were becoming a thing of the past. Unemployment levels in the central cities soared high above the national average. As the African-American sociologist William Julius Wilson would note of the urban economy in the 1990s, "For the first

I just want to do God's will. And He's allowed me to go up to the mountain. And I've looked over. And I've seen the promised land. I may not get there with you. But I want you to know tonight, that we, as a people, will get to the promised land.

◆

—Dr. Martin Luther King, Jr., 1968

time in the twentieth century most adults in many inner-city ghetto neighborhoods are not working in a typical week."

At the start of the 1960s, less than a third of America's poor lived in urban areas; by the 1990s that figure had risen to almost half of the nation's poor. In 1962 social critic Michael Harrington had written that the poor—the "other America"—were largely invisible to middle class Americans. Thirty years later that was no longer the case. The urban poor were highly concentrated, and thus also a highly visible population. The social ills that accompanied big-city poverty —crime, drug addiction, rising rates of children born out of wedlock and raised in single-parent families—became merged in the eyes of outside observers into the threatening image of an "underclass." Conservatives blamed the welfare system, liberals blamed racism or economic deprivation, but everyone agreed that life for those living in minority communities in big cities was qualitatively worse than it had been a generation earlier.

An elderly black woman living on the South Side of Chicago reminisced with an interviewer about how things had been when she first moved to the neighborhood 40 years earlier:

> I've been here since March 21, 1953. When I moved in, the neighborhood was intact. It was intact with homes, beautiful homes, mini-mansions, with stores, laundromats, with cleaners, with Chinese [cleaners]. We had drugstores. We had hotels. We had doctors over on Thirty-ninth Street. We had doctors' offices in the neighborhood. We had the middle class and upper middle class. It has gone from affluent to where it is today.

As one of William Julius Wilson's research associates commented:

The once-lively streets—residents remember a time, not so long ago, when crowds were so dense at rush hour that one had to elbow one's way to the train station—now have the appearance of an empty, bombed-out war zone. The commercial strip has been reduced to a long tunnel of charred stores, vacant lots littered with broken glass and garbage, and dilapidated buildings left to rot in the shadow of the elevated train line. At the corner of Sixty-third Street and Cottage Grove Avenue, the handful of remaining establishments that struggle to survive are huddled behind wrought-iron bars. . . . The only enterprises that seem to be thriving are liquor stores and currency exchanges, these "banks of the poor" where one can cash checks, pay bills and buy money orders for a fee.

The 1970s ushered in a new era in black migration—a "reverse migration" to the South. From 1970 to 1975, while about a quarter million southern blacks moved North, more than 300,000 northern blacks moved South, the first time that anything like that had ever happened. With the triumph of the civil rights movement in the South, the North's image as the "promised land" was in jeopardy. In 1978 *Ebony* magazine surveyed the "ten best cities for Blacks" in the United States; three of them, Atlanta, Dallas, Houston, were in the Deep South, and two more, Baltimore and Washington, had been bastions of segregation until the 1960s. In a related development, middle-class African Americans—like their white counterparts—fled the cities for the suburbs. In the 1980s nearly 50,000 blacks moved out of Washington, D.C., resulting in a decline of about 11 percent in the city's black population. Many of them moved to Prince George's County in neighboring Maryland, which by the start of the 1990s had become the first black-majority suburban county in the United States.

The men and women who boarded trains bound for Chicago and other northern cities in 1916 and 1917 and the

A *migrant mother and her child in Chicago at the beginning of the Great Migration* (from Chicago Commission on Race Relations, *The Negro in Chicago*, 1920, p. 48)

years of the Great Migration that followed turned to the language and examples of Old Testament stories to explain to themselves and to others what they were trying to accomplish. The flight of the Jews from the Land of Egypt, their pursuit of Pharaoh, their wanderings in the wilderness, their abiding faith in their God, and their eventual arrival in the land of milk and honey were among the images that sustained African Americans in their own quest for a better life in a strange new geographic and social landscape. The cities of the North did not prove to be Sweet Canaan Land. History is rarely so simple or so kind in its workings. The struggle for black equality and dignity continued in the North, vanquishing some old adversaries while having to contend with new trials and tribulations. At the end of the 20th century, the Promised Land is still at least another day's journey on.

NOTES

p. 116 "For the first time . . ." William Julius Wilson, *When Work Disappears: The World of the New Urban Poor* (New York: Alfred A. Knopf, 1996), p. xiii.

p. 117 "I've been here since . . ." Wilson, *When Work Disappears*, p. 3.

p. 118 "The once-lively streets . . ." Wilson, *When Work Disappears*, p. 5.

Bibliography and Further Reading List

History of the Great Migration

Crew, Spencer R. *Field to Factory: Afro-American Migration, 1915–1940.* Washington, D.C.: Smithsonian Institution, 1987. Well-illustrated text, designed to accompany the American Museum of Natural History's permanent exhibit on the Great Migration.

Fligstein, Neil. *Going North: Migration of Blacks and Whites from the South, 1900–1950.* New York: Academic Press, 1981. Scholarly and heavily statistical, it makes the important point that southern whites too undertook their own "great migration" in the 20th century.

Henri, Florette. *Black Migration: Movement North, 1900–1920.* Garden City, New York: Anchor Press, Doubleday, 1975. An impressive scholarly study of the Great Migration, long the standard work on the subject.

Hine, Darlene C., and Clayborne Carson, ed. *Bound for Glory: From the Great Migration to the Harlem Renaissance (1910–1930).* Broomall, Penn.: Chelsea House, 1995. Chronological exploration of the period of the Great Migration, for young adults.

Katz, William L. *Great Migrations, 1880–1912.* Chatham, N.J.: Raintree Steck-Vaughn, 1995. Young adult title.

Lawrence, Jacob. *The Great Migration: An American Story*. New York: HarperCollins, 1993. A beautiful picture book using Lawrence's series of paintings. Meant for children.

Marks, Carole. *Farewell—We're Good and Gone: The Great Black Migration*. Bloomington: Indiana University Press, 1989. Highly readable and perceptive overview of the Great Migration.

Scott, Emmett J. *Negro Migration During the War*. New York: Oxford University Press, 1920. One of the first studies published about the Great Migration, rich in detail.

Trotter, Joe William, Jr., ed. *The Great Migration in Historical Perspective*. Bloomington: Indiana University Press, 1991. Essays by leading scholars in the field; a good indicator of current historical debates and focuses.

Studies of Particular Cities

The Chicago Commission on Race Relations. *The Negro in Chicago: A Study of Race Relations and a Race Riot*. Chicago: University of Chicago Press, 1922. Richly detailed and illustrated primary source on the Great Migration and its impact on Chicago.

Drake, St. Clair, and Horace R. Cayton. *Black Metropolis: A Study of Negro Life in a Northern City*. New York: Harcourt, Brace, and World, 1962. An updated reprint of the classic 1945 study of the growth of black Chicago.

Gottlieb, Peter. *Making Their Own Way: Southern Blacks' Migration to Pittsburgh, 1916–30*. Urbana: University of Illinois Press, 1987. A fine scholarly study of the Great Migration's impact on this industrial center.

Grossman, James R. *Land of Hope: Chicago, Black Southerners, and the Great Migration*. Chicago: University of Chicago Press, 1989. Well illustrated, scholarly, and lively. If you read only one additional book on the subject, this should be it.

Kusmer, Kenneth. *A Ghetto Takes Shape: Black Cleveland, 1870–1930*. Urbana: University of Illinois Press, 1976. Good scholarly study of Cleveland's black community.

Martin, Elizabeth Anne. *Detroit and the Great Migration, 1916–1929*. Ann Arbor: University of Michigan, 1993. Short, well-illustrated history of Detroit in the Great Migration.

Osofsky, Gilbert. *Harlem: The Making of a Ghetto, 1890–1930*. New York: Harper Torchbooks, 1963. This was a pioneering work in the history of northern black communities.

Schomburg Center for Research in Black Culture. *Harlem, 1900–1929: Spiritual Home of Black America*. New York: New York Public

Library, 1974. An exhibit portfolio reproducing several dozen striking images of life in what became in this period the most important center of urban African-American life.

Spear, Allan. *Black Chicago: The Making of a Negro Ghetto, 1890–1920*. Chicago: University of Chicago Press, 1967. A first-rate scholarly study of the Chicago black community.

Trotter, Jr., Joe William. *Black Milwaukee: The Making of an Industrial Proletariat*. Urbana: University of Illinois Press, 1985. Trotter offers a workplace rather than a community focus in his study of black Milwaukee, bringing an important new dimension to histories of the Great Migration and its aftermath.

Related Topics

DuBois, W. E. B.. *The Philadelphia Negro; a social study*. New York: Schocken Books, 1967. A classic study of what was in the years before the Great Migration the largest black community in the North.

Jones, Jacqueline. *The Dispossessed: America's Underclasses from the Civil War to the Present*. New York: Basic Books, 1992. A passionate study of the lives of the black and white American poor over the past century by a leading American scholar, with several chapters focusing on the Great Migration and its aftermath.

Harris, William H. *The Harder We Run: Black Workers Since the Civil War*. New York: Oxford University Press, 1982. An excellent overview of African-American experience in the workplace and the labor movement.

Litwack, Leon F. *Been in the Storm So Long: The Aftermath of Slavery*. New York: Alfred A. Knopf, 1979. A richly detailed account of southern African-American life in the decade following emancipation, including a chapter on black migration within the postwar South.

———. *North of Slavery: The Negro in the Free States, 1790–1860*. Chicago: University of Chicago Press, 1961. This is the standard work on African Americans in the North a century before the Great Migration.

Lomax, Alan. *Land Where the Blues Began*. New York: Pantheon Books, 1993. A highly personal, engrossing, and knowledgeable account of the rural southern blues and their impact on American culture in the 20th century.

McKissack, Patricia and Fredrick. *W. E. B. DuBois*. Danbury, Conn.: Franklin Watts, 1991. Award-winning biography for young adults.

McPherson, James M. *Marching Toward Freedom: Blacks in the Civil War, 1861–1865*. New York: Facts On File, 1991. This is an easy-to-read overview of the contribution by black soldiers to emancipation, written by a leading scholar in the field for young adults.

Painter, Nell Irvin. *Exodusters: Black Migration to Kansas After Reconstruction*. New York: Alfred A. Knopf, 1976. A fine historical study of the first major migration to the North of ex-slaves.

Tushnet, Mark V. *Brown v. Board of Education: The Battle for Integration*. Danbury, Conn.: Franklin Watts, 1995. Book written for young adults on this landmark court case.

Tuttle, William M. *Race Riot: Chicago in the Red Summer of 1919*. New York: Atheneum, 1970. A scholarly, readable, and sobering account of racial violence in the midst of the Great Migration.

Wepman, Dennis. *The Struggle for Freedom: African-American Slave Resistance*. New York: Facts On File, 1996. This is an overview written for young adults of the history of African-American resistance to slavery.

Aftermath of the Great Migration

Hirsch, Arnold R. *Making the Second Ghetto: Race and Housing in Chicago, 1940–1960*. Scholarly study of discrimination in residential housing during and after the Second World War.

Kleppner, Paul. *Chicago Divided: The Making of a Black Mayor*. DeKalb: Northern Illinois University Press, 1985. Scholarly study of the demographic and political changes that led to the election of Harold Washington as Chicago's Mayor in 1983.

Kotlowitz, Alex. *There Are No Children Here: The Story of Two Boys Growing Up in the Other America*. New York: Anchor Books, 1992. A harrowing journalistic account of life in Chicago's projects.

Lemann, Nicholas. *The Promised Land: The Great Black Migration and How It Changed America*. New York: Alfred A. Knopf, 1991. A first-rate though controversial account of the post–World War II black migration from Mississippi to Chicago, by a leading American journalist.

Rivlin, Gary. *Fire on the Prairie: Chicago's Harold Washington and the Politics of Race*. New York: Henry Holt and Company, 1992. A journalist's account of the rise of black political power in Chicago.

Index

Italic page numbers indicate illustrations.

Rome, Georgia 56
Roosevelt, Franklin Delano 104, 105, 106, 109, 115
Rutgers University 99

S

St. George Methodist Church (Philadelphia) 35
St. Louis, Missouri 65
Salem Baptist Church (Chicago) 87
Sandburg, Carl 38, 71
San Francisco, California 109, 110
Savannah, Georgia 48
Scott, Emmett 52
Scott, Mississippi 98
Seattle, Washington 109
segregation 1–3, 16–17, 29–30, 37, 75, 111, 112–13, 118 *See also* Jim Crow laws
    in the army 43
Selma, Alabama 113
"separate but equal" 17
settlement houses 32–34
sharecroppers 11–12, 111
Shelley v. Kraemer 78
slavery 3–6, 7, 10, *11*, 19, 20, 21, 23, 28, 29, 35, 59, 78
Smith, Al 105
Smith, Bessie 98
Smith, Clara 98–99
Smith, Mamie 97
Souls of Black Folk, The (DuBois) 5, 19, 33
South Carolina 4, 8, 10, 17, 64
Spanish-American War 41
Steinbeck, John 107
Stillman House (New York City) 34
Stockyard Labor Council 76
Supreme Court, U.S. 17, 78, 111
"Sweet Canaan's happy land" 5

T

Taft, William Howard 105
Tennessee 2
Terrell, Mary Church 34
Texas 4, 64
Thirteenth Amendment 12

Thompson, William ("Big Bill") Hale 71, 82
369th U.S. Infantry 90–91
Toomer, Jean 96
trade unions *See* Unions
Trenton, New Jersey 65
"Tuskegee Machine" 15
Tuskegee Institute 14, 51

U

Underground Railroad 5, 25, 59
Unemployment Councils 104
unions 28–31, 33, 74–77, 94, 105, 109, 116
United States 3, 7, 14, 23, 29, 40, 41, 44, 118
United States Employment Service (USES) 46, 109
Universal Negro Improvement Association (UNIA) 101–2
University of Atlanta 33
University of Berlin 32
University of Pennsylvania 32
Up from Slavery (Washington) 14
Urban League 34, 46, *55*, 63, *63*, 71–73, *72*, 77, 95

V

Vann, Robert 106
Veterans Administration 115
Virginia 3, 4, 14, 64
voting rights 7, 9, 13, 16, 21, 71, 86, 114

W

War Department, U.S. 52
War Manpower Commission 109
War Production Board 109
Washington, Booker T. 14–15, 17, 33, 48, 51, 52, 53–54, 101
Washington, Harold 112–13
Washington, D.C. 24, 34, 65, 66, 85, 105, 113, 114, 118
Waters, Ethel 98
Watts riot 114
welfare system 117